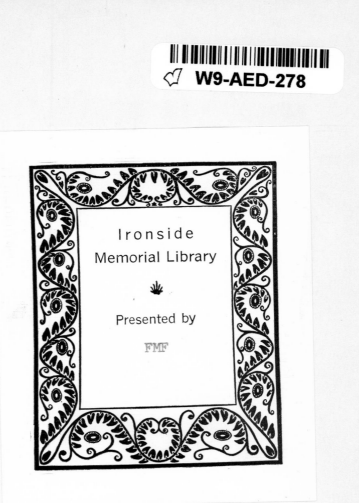

Ironside
Memorial Library

Presented by

FMF

MAN'S PEACE   GOD'S GLORY

IVP *Series in Creative Christian Living*

MAN'S PEACE   GOD'S GLORY

ERIC S. FIFE

INTER-VARSITY PRESS

Cover design by Gordon H. Stromberg

Printed in the United States of America

2442

Foreword

THE INITIAL SURGE of missionary concern among college and university students during the decade following World War II has ebbed in recent years. Fewer volunteers are available for service overseas, yet the need for young men and women to serve their Lord in a variety of positions is constantly increasing. Today's students need a clear presentation of the biblical basis of missions—motivated by a concern for the glory of God, as well as the need of man, and characterized by a sane, warm, practical approach.

Mr. Eric Fife, Missionary Director of the Inter-Varsity Christian Fellowship, is well qualified for this task. During World War II he served with the Royal Air Force in North Africa where he developed a deep concern for the Moslem world. Upon his return to England he went into a pastoral ministry, but continued his active interest in the missionary task of the Church through service on the Home Council of the North Africa Mission. In 1954 the author came to the United States as Deputation Secretary for this mission. In the years following, his ministry among college students in conferences and campus visits increased. In 1957 he was invited to become Missionary Director of the Inter-Varsity Christian Fellowship, which includes the Student Foreign Missions Fellowship.

Out of these years of varied experience Mr. Fife writes—primarily for college and university students who are Christians. He keeps in mind the many students who are relatively new in the Faith since coming to the campus. Yet this new book on missions should prove helpful to a much wider circle of Christians who desire not only to know the principles involved but also to have them operative in daily living.

The IVCF presents *Man's Peace, God's Glory* with the prayer that it may be used by God to kindle in the hearts of many of His people, especially students at the threshhold of their vocation, a burning concern for the fulfillment of the Great Commission.

CHARLES E. HUMMEL
Field Director
Inter-Varsity Christian Fellowship

Preface

In this book, as in all my ministry, I have endeavored to accomplish three things: (1) to encourage the reader to study the Bible for himself; (2) to present the need for world evangelism and the responsibility of each Christian for this task; and (3) to offer devotional truths with personal application.

The third purpose will be most obvious in the later chapters of the book, though it pervades the whole. I believe it to be extremely important, for without it a "foreign missions emphasis" can easily become a hobby horse rather than a way of life.

At the time of writing, there are more than three and a half million students in colleges in the United States of America alone. To a large extent an adequate supply of overseas missionaries will depend upon our ability to inform Christian students of their privilege and responsibility toward God and His purposes. There are many signs of a rising tide of missionary interest on the campuses of our secular schools. And even though it will be several years before their training is completed and these students are available for service, we are thankful for this trend. If this book does even a small amount to strengthen and develop that interest, I shall have been more than repaid for the labor involved.

ERIC S. FIFE
Missionary Director
Inter-Varsity Christian Fellowship

Contents

Man's Peace God's Glory

"THE GREAT PRACTICAL PROBLEM whose solution demands the prayerful and prompt attention of every believer is this: How may the Church of Christ carry the good tidings round the world during the lifetime of this generation? For the present generation of the saved to reach the present generation of the unsaved is the one question of the hour that leaves all others far in the distance. To the solution of that problem in God's own way, the Church, and every member of it, should bring all the brains, heart, conscience, will, money, intelligence or enterprise at command."

ARTHUR T. PIERSON

Chapter 1: **Introduction**

It was a sunday morning in the summer of 1945. The sun was shining brightly, and even the English Channel was in a benign mood. Life was very pleasant, especially for the hundreds of men on the "Georgic," luxury liner turned troopship, as it cut its way through the water, homeward bound for England.

True, the ship was crowded. But who cared when, after absences of several years and more, the men were within hours of setting their feet on English soil once again?

Suddenly there was an outburst of noise and excitement, and I made my way forward to see what it was all about. There I discovered, conspicuous among the British troops, a small group of thirty or forty French sailors who had fought with the Free French forces in the Mediterranean. All were gesticulating wildly and shouting, "Vive la France." The cause of the uproar was immediately discernible as I saw the coast of Brittany, looking serene and beautiful in the distance on the right-hand side of the ship.

A few, almost unbearably long hours passed, and there at last was the shore of England itself—the tiny, unbelievably green fields that seemed to tumble over the magnificent white Cornish cliffs in an attempt to welcome us home.

Inevitably, my mind slipped back over the events of the past twenty-eight months since I had left the blacked-out shores of England, ignorant of the destination and doubtful of return. The intervening months had not been uneventful ones. There came almost too vividly to mind the time when a bomb-laden airplane had exploded, destroying eighteen other aircraft, yet miraculously leaving me unharmed though only a few yards away. The time when after a highway crash I had lain for thirty minutes on a road in Tunisia with my head trapped under an overturned truck until my rescuers were able to jack up the truck and extricate me. The time when, flying in a single-engine aircraft, we had plunged toward the ground with a dead motor, only to have it burst into life just in time to permit a safe landing.

Certainly God had been good and, having been preserved, I wondered what purpose He had for my life in the future. Surely I wanted it to count for Him.

It was impossible to think of the future without thinking of the past. In succeeding months as I gave thought to the question of a career, I had always as a background an impression of 23,000,000 Muslims living on the southern shore of the Mediterranean Sea, wedged in between the ocean and the Sahara Desert, indifferent to Jesus Christ and almost untouched so far

14

as effective missionary work was concerned. Often in those days I saw again the tiny, frail form of Mlle. Butticaz, who gave so much of her life to serve the Lord in the little oasis of Bou Saada. When I had left Algiers her words had been: "I will pray that some day God will bring you back to this country as a missionary."

I was willing to go back, but the Lord did not lead in that direction. He had other plans, but certainly my attitude toward the idea of foreign missionary service was a very real test of my willingness to be obedient to the Lord. I could say very honestly that, even though the prospect of missionary service in North Africa was not an appealing one, I was willing to go.

Willing to go?

It seemed a perfectly normal and satisfactory response to the missionary challenge at that time. Yet, even though I have no doubt that the Lord has overruled every detail and that I am in the place of His appointment, I have come to feel very strongly that "to be willing" is a feeble, anemic, flaccid response to the demands of the Lord and of the world. The flabbiness of this response stands in startling distinction to the attitude of the Apostle Paul.

"I am willing that Israel might be saved"? No. Rather, "I could wish that I myself were accursed and cut off from Christ for the sake of my brethren" (Romans 9:3). "Woe to me if I do not preach the gospel!" (I Corinthians 9:16). "I am eager to preach the gospel to you also who are in Rome" (Romans 1:15).

15

The Apostle Paul's desire "to make all men see" (Ephesians 3:9) was not an optional extra or a half-hearted offer of service, wrung from a reluctant servant. It was the wholehearted, eager response of a soul fired with a sense of gratitude and a deep sense of privilege because God had committed to him a part in this glad service.

Some years ago, through no fault of my own, I came to be in debt. My mother had died and such slender worldly wealth as was hers was delivered to my keeping, since she had appointed me the executor for her estate. Along with this property came a will that contained clear and specific instructions as to what was to be done with the money. So much was to go to my eldest brother, so much to my second brother, so much to my third brother, and so much to myself.

I received the inheritance, but even though I was to benefit from it, I had a duty to discharge to others. As long as the money was in my possession I was in debt. It was not a matter of my generosity or magnanimity; neither did it depend upon my inclination. Rather it was an obligation laid upon me by law.

When Paul wrote to the Romans, "I am a debtor" (Romans 1:14), it was more than an interesting phrase; it summed up his whole philosophy of life. He was a man in debt. In Jesus Christ he had received the greatest inheritance that any man can ever receive. But along with this blessing came instructions just as clear and specific as those that I received in my mother's last will and testament: he was appointed to share this bounty with the Jews and Gentiles, barbarians and free, wise and foolish. And this became the mission and passion of his life.

Contrast Paul's attitude with the easygoing approach that characterizes so many of us in the Church of Christ today. The gospel, we feel, is not a debt to be discharged, but rather a gratuity to be bestowed if the circumstances are favorable and we happen to be in the mood. Yet world evangelization should not be the hobby of a few enthusiasts, but the glad duty of every member of the Church of Christ. When we accepted the blessings of salvation, we accepted (whether we knew it or not) the obligation to share this blessing with every nation, "to the uttermost parts of the earth."

Whether God takes us to another country or we remain at home, whether we are in so-called full-time or part-time service, whether we are called to preach or to be a housewife, at this point, is irrelevant. God's commission is binding upon each one of us.

Students often write to me and confess a lack of missionary passion:

I went to a missionary conference and the Lord spoke to me about foreign missions. He put a real burden on my heart, but after a few weeks I found that my concern and enthusiasm had evaporated. What is wrong with me that I can be so unconcerned and what can I do to remedy this? This has happened to me again and again.

Letters like this are a common occurrence.

How much missionary passion should we have? Should we have a missionary passion at all?

We need to remind ourselves that "missionary passion" is not a scriptural term. Passion is an emotion, and the feeling and expression of emotion vary tremendously from one temperament to another. My passion about world missions may vary a great deal—it is hard to feel passion with a migraine headache or a heavy head cold—but my conviction about world missions should be unwavering.

We respond to the Lord's commands by our wills. Usually God reaches our wills through our emotions, or through our minds, or through both. The fact that I was profoundly moved at a meeting does not mean that that emotional feeling should necessarily continue. Neither, on the other hand, does it mean that it was necessarily wrong. It does mean that it ought to lead to some positive, definite action on my part. For although I will not be judged according to how I *feel* about missions, I will be judged according to how I *act* about missions.

Most of us do not have Paul's commitment to the task of evangelizing the world and are prepared to admit that we don't. How can we develop a real missionary vision for ourselves and among our Christian friends?

The first step is to tell the Lord honestly that we do not share His concern for His world and ask Him to

18

give us something of the love and urgency of His own heart. This is a prayer the Lord delights to answer.

The second step is to gain information from God himself. We need to be clear about God's purpose for His world—and we can be, for He has revealed much of it in His Word. In fact, the whole of the Bible from Genesis to Revelation is supremely concerned with God's purpose for this world. As we consider this subject together through the pages of this book, may God move us *by His truth*. For unless our convictions are squarely based upon the Scripture, they cannot be really enduring or pleasing to God.

The third step is to gain a perspective on the world. When John Wesley was asked why he read the newspaper, he replied, "To see what my God is doing in the world." We cannot know what God is doing unless we know His Word and His world. We shall not have room here for discussion of the world situations or conditions on the foreign field; that must wait for a further book. But let us learn to relate all our reading to God's purpose in the world.

If we lack the single-minded dedication of Paul, before we go any further let us be sure that we take the first of the three steps and prepare to take the other two. For our attitude as we begin a study such as this is of great importance.

The purpose of this book is that together we may see in the Bible something of God's purposes in the world—how we are involved and what contribution we can

19

make. In succeeding pages we shall see something of
how God's concern for the whole world was recorded
in the Old Testament, as well as in the New Testament. We shall observe that Jesus Christ was highly
specific in His teaching about the evangelization of the
world and how the apostolic Church implemented His
commission. We shall consider the true bases of missionary vision and the true motive for missionary service. We shall move on to the subject of prayer and
giving and finally to missionary qualifications. In our
consideration of these truths, our attitude toward them
may determine the results of our study together.

Chapter 2: **The Need of Man and the Purpose of God**

What is wrong with the world?

Few people need to be convinced that *something* is wrong. Events around the world indicate vividly that all is not well. Hungary, Suez, Algeria, Cuba, the Congo, Formosa, China, India, Korea—each name brings to mind tension, crisis, fear and death.

But we need not look across the seas for evidence that something is wrong. In the United States itself there is tragic discord: labor–management tensions, political and civic corruption, racial unrest, juvenile delinquency, divorce and broken homes. One-tenth of the people in the United States need treatment for emotional or mental disorders. One-twentieth will spend time in a mental institution. Most of us do not need to look outside our own lives to find tension, fear and disharmony.

What is wrong with the world?

There have been many attempts to find the answer. Some have looked to politics and government, trying to put their finger on the problem and then evolve from these fields a solution. At first sight, this approach seems to be a hopeful one. After all, it is government that produces order out of chaos, that restrains law-breakers in the interest of common good, that makes for prosperity. And yet the closer we get to politics and government, the more certain we are that the complete answer is not in this realm.

So often governments, even good strong governments, find themselves in the grip of circumstances they cannot control. A government cannot rule without power, but "power corrupts, and absolute power corrupts absolutely," whether that power be vested in a king, a party, or a dictatorship. After centuries of every conceivable form of government, the twentieth century has laid bare the fact that no government can provide the answer, for no government can be stronger than the people who govern, or the people who are governed.

Others have felt that the problem is ignorance and that the answer is education. As we see the terrible effects of ignorance in underdeveloped areas (particularly ignorance of health standards) and the blessings brought by education, a wave of optimism sweeps over us, until we think again. If this were the trouble, the only trouble, and education were the answer, the complete answer, we would expect that the centers of higher learning would be the places of greatest dedication to the common good and the highest degree of morality, happiness, and harmony. But no person who spends time in such centers today can believe that this is true of them.

22

Communism has insisted that education can change man's innate selfishness and make him regard the welfare of others and of the state as more important than his own welfare. But this concept has been exploded by Milovan Djilas in *The New Class*.

Marx observed that tension is unavoidable so long as there are "haves" and "have nots." He saw economic injustice as the "villain of the peace." An equality of wealth, property, position and opportunity would cure finally the ills that have plagued the human race for so long, he thought.

Smug and comfortable indeed must be the person who fails to see the element of truth in this reasoning. Inequality *does* breed bitterness, injustice *does* breed hatred. If we are too stupid, too self-centered, too self-satisfied to see this in the racial tensions in the United States, or in the longing for independence in Africa and Asia, we shall learn the hard way in coming years and pay a deep price for the education.

But this is not the whole truth. If it were, those who have most of this world's goods would be exempt from tensions and would hold the key to happiness and harmony, at least in this life. But divorce court proceedings and medical reports sound the death knell for this view. I remember being driven around the plushiest section of a city in the Midwest, admiring the beautiful homes with three-car garages, wonderful views overlooking Lake Michigan, and private beaches. My guide, who knew the district intimately, commented, "I hap-

23

pen to know that there is hardly a home here that does not know tragedy of one kind or another—divorce, alcoholism, suicide, criminal children, etc." We may shut the door on poverty but we cannot shut out discord and trouble, for that is bound up in the life of man.

What *is* wrong with the world? To find the answer we need to turn, not to politics, economics or education, but to the Bible.

On one occasion when I attended a performance of Handel's "Messiah," the auditorium was plunged into darkness because of a power failure. Immediately the chorus and orchestra lapsed into discord. They could not see the conductor. Similarly, man who does not see God—who neither trusts nor follows Him—is out of harmony with God. This is what is wrong with the world.

When a government loses its control through war or revolution, law and order come to an end; anarchy prevails. Human life and property are constantly in danger.

When an army is cut off from its base, the consequent loss of communications and leadership leads inevitably to irresolution and incohesiveness. The ability to perform as a fighting force is destroyed. So it is with man cut off from God.

God created man and gave him unique authority:

> Thou hast given him dominion over the works of thy
> hands;
> thou hast put all things under his feet,
> all sheep and oxen,

24

and also the beasts of the field,
the birds of the air, and the fish of the sea,
whatever passes along the paths of the sea.
(Psalm 8:6-8)

God gave man authority but demanded that man, in turn, should accept the authority of God himself.

A Tunisian student once prayed one of the most cynical prayers ever uttered: "O God, give me holiness, but not yet." At sixteen he was the father of an illegitimate son. Yet he lived to write the most succinct summary of man's experience apart from God: "Thou hast created us for Thyself and our hearts are restless until they find their rest in Thee." The name of that student was Augustine. He lived 1600 years ago, but his statement is true today as it was true then.

Man has rebelled against the authority of God and rejected His dominion. In doing so, he has cut himself off from the only source of peace and harmony, God himself. The tension, the unrest, the conflict within human society is but the reflection of the tension and the conflict that is within the heart of man himself. ". . . your iniquities have made a separation between you and your God . . ." (Isaiah 59:2).

But God has a purpose and He has explained what it is.

Praise be to God for giving us every possible spiritual benefit in Christ! For consider what He has done— before the foundation of the world He chose us to become, in Christ, His holy and blameless children living within His constant care. He planned, in His purpose of love, that we should be adopted as His own children through Jesus Christ—that we might learn to praise that glorious generosity of His which has made us welcome to the everlasting love He bears towards the Son. It is through the Son, at the cost of His own blood, that we are redeemed, freely forgiven through that full and generous grace which has overflowed into our lives and opened our eyes to the truth. For God has allowed us to know the secret of His Plan, and it is this: He purposes in His sovereign will that all human history shall be consummated in Christ, that everything that exists in Heaven or earth shall find its perfection and fulfilment in Him. And here is the staggering thing—that in all which will one day belong to Him we have been promised a share (since we were long ago destined for this by the One Who achieves His purposes by His sovereign Will), so that we, as the first to put our confidence in Christ, may bring praise to His glory! And you too trusted Him, when you had heard the message of truth, the Gospel of your salvation. And after you gave your confidence to Him you were, so to speak, stamped with the promised Holy Spirit as a guarantee of purchase, until the day when God completes the redemption of what He has paid for as his own; and that will again be to the praise of His glory" (Ephesians 1:3-14, from *The New Testament in Modern English,* © J. B. Phillips 1958. Used by permission of The Macmillan Company).

This is a tremendous passage of Scripture that might well be expounded thoroughly. But note just three or four truths that stand out and are particularly pertinent to our subject.

The first: God has a purpose in the world. The Scriptures say again and again that God has a purpose in this world and that no force of earth or hell can frustrate or defeat it. "Surely the wrath of man shall praise thee" (Psalm 76:10). We need to grasp the fact that neither the wisdom and power of His adversaries, nor even the foolishness and weakness of His disciples will prevent the Lord from working out His plan to His eternal glory. In a world of apparent disorder and chaos, when so often we seem to be at the mercy of the forces of evil, it is a tremendous source of strength to recognize that God has a purpose and that nothing will prevent that purpose from being worked out.

The second truth is that the center, the pivot of God's purpose is Jesus Christ himself. Any plan or program of the Church in which the organization or plan itself has more prominence than the purpose of Christ is alien to the entire spirit of the New Testament. The purpose of God will have its final and its complete consummation in Christ.

The third fact is that God's purpose, although centered in Christ, involves men. God's purpose involves not only exceptional men, but ordinary men; not only good men, but sinful men. This is clearly seen in the second chapter of Ephesians, where Paul describes for his readers what they were like before they became Christians. We must see what God's purpose is for the

27

men whom He chooses. What was God's purpose for those men at Ephesus? What is God's purpose for you? What is God's purpose for me? It does not say that it is to be successful, or popular (we need to remember this today). Nor does it say even that it is to be useful. God's purpose is that they and we "should be holy and blameless before him" (Ephesians 1:4).

The fourth truth is that God's purpose is to reveal God's glory, to result in "the praise of His glory." I may be a good missionary doctor and yet not glorify Him. I may be a fine Christian educator and yet not glorify Him. I can go to extraordinary lengths of sacrifice and self-denial, yet fail to bring glory to Him. We may double and treble our missionary force, yet fail to glorify Him. I may be a successful student, or be active in a missionary program, yet fail to bring "praise to His glory." I may be bringing far more praise to my own glory.

A man may work for forty years in some obscure corner of the world and be a complete failure as far as the world counts success, and often so far as the Church tends to count success today, too. But if he has lived a life that shows triumph over sin, if he is reflecting something of the glory and the grace of Jesus Christ, he will have been an outstanding success so far as God is concerned, because he is working in accord with the revealed purpose of God for His Church.

We are accustomed to evaluate the success of a business by its balance sheet, the success of a school by its

28

enrollment and academic achievement, the success of a business man by the wealth and position he acquires. It is natural for us to use this method of evaluation in the Lord's work. It is natural. That is precisely our trouble. Our judgment is a natural judgment as opposed to a spiritual one. Our evaluation is a natural evaluation, and the Scripture tells us that the natural or unspiritual man does not receive the things of God (I Corinthians 2:14). And II Corinthians 4:18 reminds us that visible things are temporal, transient; whereas only invisible things are eternal. But because we are human the visible has a great fascination for us. This is just as real in the Lord's work as it is in our own private lives. The longing to justify ourselves and our work, the drive to succeed which is based in pride, constitute much of the motivating power of our so-called Christian service.

When a missionary is asked what he is trying to do, what his goals are, what he is working to accomplish, he usually has a ready answer. In some cases we have not really thought through these answers. Instead of giving an ultimate, basic objective, we state secondary objectives. We have been working so hard at the means that we have tended to substitute them for the end. There are some Christians who talk as if the object of foreign missions is to produce literature that equals in quality and quantity the output of Soviet Russia. There are others who talk as if our goals should be to surpass the cults in their zeal and in their proselytizing, as if we should expect to get adherents as rapidly as they do. We do need to produce literature and we should have zeal in evangelization. But these are not the basic objectives.

What is the role of the Church in the twentieth century? Is it to build bigger hospitals, develop more effective systems of Christian education, build more powerful radio transmitters, fly more airplanes, penetrate more tribes, reduce more languages to writing? Each of these goals is good; in fact, each of these goals is or may be inherent in the Church's role today. But none of them *is* that role. None by itself constitutes the goal of the Church of Christ today. Our great danger is that each one of these can become an end in itself.

What is the purpose of the Church of Christ? If this question had been asked some years ago, probably most evangelical Christians would have answered by saying, "The purpose of the Church is to save souls." But, fortunately, we have managed to progress beyond this today. If the same question were posed today, probably many thoughtful Christians would say, "It is to save souls and to build indigenous churches." Now this is a tremendous improvement. But does it adequately summarize the purpose of the Church of Christ?

Let us assume for a moment that this is the purpose of the Church. Let us test the ministry of Samuel Zwemer by this purpose. Zwemer worked for some twenty-five years in Arabia and in Egypt among the Muslims. Because of the difficulties of work among

30

Muslims, there were probably no more than seven converts. If God's plan for Samuel Zwemer was that he should win souls, and His judgment was in terms of the *number* of souls won, Zwemer's life could hardly be called a success. Or, if the goal of the ministry of Zwemer was to establish indigenous churches, his life was a complete failure. Some may reply that Samuel Zwemer was an exception. Yet we have to remember that his experience has been duplicated a thousand times the world over by other missionaries working among Muslims and in other particularly unresponsive areas among other unresponsive people. To win souls and establish churches is certainly the will of God. Woe to the church or the Christian who is careless or indifferent about this. But, important as these are, they are not the basic, ultimate purpose of the Church of Jesus Christ.

Failure to understand these truths means that we shall never understand the program of God in the world. God's purpose is not mainly the well-being of man; it is the glory of God. Of course God is concerned with man, "For God so loved the world that he gave his only Son, that whoever believes in him should not perish but have eternal life" (John 3:16). God is concerned with man. But that is not His prime concern. The real concern of God is to reveal himself to the world, to reveal His glory in the world.

Historically, God has usually been glorified, not through large numbers of people who profess to know

31

Him, but rather through a relatively small group of people who truly live according to His will. His aim is to reveal His glory. This is accomplished less by quantity than it is by quality.

God is holy. He is seeking to reveal His holiness. He cannot do that through unholy Christians, however many of them there are. Suppose in a city there is a group of ten disunited Christians, living lives of carnality, worldliness and self-indulgence. Can God adequately reveal himself through those people? Suppose you increase the number from ten to a hundred of the same quality of Christians. Do we see any more of the holiness, the glory, and the righteousness of God simply because there are more of them?

God's plan is to destroy sin and to create a people of righteousness. Ultimately this plan will come to completion and perfection. We long for that day, the day when all evil will be abolished, when God's people will not merely see Him but be like Him, living in a new heaven and a new earth in which nothing but good shall live. We look for that day when this purpose of God will be ultimately and perfectly fulfilled.

But, in the meantime, God is working out His plan in part, purifying the lives of believers, creating a people of righteousness, making them more and more like himself. God is calling men and women to live holy lives.

Is it not a remarkable and a wonderful thing that God should have chosen us to be laborers in His harvest, that He should have entrusted to you and to me the proclamation of His gospel? Do we feel more and more with the Apostle Paul, "To me, though I am the very least of all the saints, this grace was given, to preach to the Gentiles the unsearchable riches of Christ . . ." (Ephesians 3:8)? More and more we need to be enthralled by the wonder of our calling to be stewards of the mystery of the gospel. We need a sense of awe that an almighty God should stoop to use us in His service to be fellow-laborers with Him.

Yet, what is even more remarkable, what is even a greater privilege is that He has chosen us, not merely to be His servants and His fellow-laborers, but to be His sons—holy and blameless before Him in love, conformed to the image of Christ, living to the praise of His glory.

What a wonderful picture Scripture gives us of the love of God lavished upon you and me. He looked upon us and He loved us. When we were without strength, He said to us, "Live." He set His love upon us and chose us. He destined us to be His sons. He brought us into His family. He gave us His name. He legally adopted us into the household of God, making us joint-heirs with Christ. The Apostle Paul comes back to this truth repeatedly—the thrill of being adopted by God and of being able to call Him "Abba, Father."

Paul says in the fifth chapter of Ephesians, verse 1: "Therefore be imitators of God as beloved children." Because you are the children of God, you ought to be

33

like God. Why? Because a child normally will show at least some of the characteristics of his parents. For instance, although my father died when I was just fourteen months old, so that I had scarcely seen him, my mother would say to me occasionally through the years, "That's a mannerism of your father's! That's just the expression your father used to have on his face." Though I hadn't consciously imitated him, I was like him. I knew, and others knew, I was my father's son. I was a partaker of his nature, just as the Scripture tells us we are partakers of the divine nature.

"Now," says the Apostle Paul, "because you are the sons of God, you ought to be like God." And not merely because we are partakers of His nature, but because we imitate those with whom we have the most to do and whom we admire. Those of us who have children know how our children imitate us, how our own expressions come back to us from our children. And if we are living in daily communion with the Lord, we should be becoming more and more like Him. "But we all, with open face beholding as in a glass the glory of the Lord, are changed into the same image from glory to glory" (II Corinthians 3:18).

Of course, it is God's will that souls should be saved. Woe to me if I am indifferent to my responsibility in bringing others to know Him. As a matter of fact, I feel increasingly the need in my own life of praying more earnestly that God will use me in His work of seeking and saving those who are lost without Him.

34

I am conscious that only God can save a soul and that only He knows who is going to be saved. This thinking puts the emphasis more upon what God can do and less upon what I can do; it is more theocentric than anthropocentric. This means that the test of my Christian service is not how busy I am, or how many people I witness to, or how many decisions I have registered.

The Lord is glorified when a person is truly saved and bears unmistakably the stamp of Christ. But I have known of some men living in immorality who were nevertheless used to bring others to God. All this proves is that the power of God is greater than even the sin of man. It may also suggest that the sins we accept in ourselves are just as detrimental to God's use of us as the sins we reject in others.

God's purpose is to establish churches. We need to remember, however, that it is possible to establish groups that are self-supporting and self-propagating, yet that fail to bring glory to God. There is nothing distinctively Christian in the indigenous principle per se. The communists have been establishing self-supporting, self-propagating, self-governing groups for years all over the world.

It is commonly said that revival is brought about by the intercession of God's people. I have real reservations about this statement. I know of some places where Christians have been praying for revival for many, many years with no apparent results. I believe there is a great deal of evidence, both in the Scriptures and in

35

history, that the basis of revival is less intercession than
it is repentance. The hallmark of genuine revival always
seems to be a deep conviction of sin; in fact, it seems to
be the prerequisite of any true, deep spiritual blessing.

It is when the Church gets concerned about its sin,
its lack of holiness, its lack of spiritual power, and con-
fesses it to the Lord that there seems to be a movement
of God in revival. It is not by chance that Isaiah, after a
vision of the glory of God, said, ". . . I saw the Lord
sitting upon a throne, high and lifted up; and his train
filled the temple . . . And one (seraphim) called to
another and said: 'Holy, holy, holy is the Lord of
hosts . . .' " (Isaiah 6:1, 3). Then he confessed his sin:
"Woe is me! For I am lost; for I am a man of unclean
lips, and I dwell in the midst of a people of unclean
lips" (Isaiah 6:5). Isaiah longed for a ministry: "Here
I am! Send me" (Isaiah 6:8).

If the glory of God fills our minds, a sense of our
own sinfulness will fill our hearts. This is basic to personal revival and to revival within the Church of
Christ. "Ye are a chosen generation . . . that ye should
show forth the praises of him who hath called you out
of darkness into his marvelous light." The test of our
Christianity and missionary service must be not, "What
am I doing?", "How much am I doing?", or "How
successful am I?", but "Am I showing forth the praises
of Him who has called me from darkness into His marvelous light?"

There are questions we must ask ourselves. First of

all, am I concerned that the glory of God might be revealed throughout all the world? This was the burden of the Apostle Paul. This was the burden of the Psalmist in the ninety-sixth Psalm:

> Declare his glory among the nations,
> his marvelous works among all the peoples!
> . . . .
> Say among the nations, "The Lord reigns! . . ."
> . . . .
> For all the gods of the peoples are idols;
> but the Lord made the heavens.
> (Psalm 96:3, 10, 5)

Do you have any real concern that the glory of God should be revealed throughout the world?

The second question we need to ask ourselves is this: "What am I doing to see that the glory of God is spread throughout the world?" I may be immersed in my studies or absorbed in my Christian service, and lack the vision of a world half of which has never even heard "that God has made this Jesus both Lord and Christ." What is my contribution to world evangelism? What is yours? What is our contribution to seeing that the glory of God is spread throughout all the world?

The third question we must ask is this: "Is there in my life a quality of motive, a quality of service, above all else a quality of living that will bring praise to the glory of God?" If, as we consider these things, we are aware of falling short of what God wants us to be, we must not attempt to manufacture these graces ourselves.

37

We might just as well try to manufacture an apple or an orange as to manufacture a spiritual grace. Only God can do that. Spiritual grace is a fruit of spiritual life, just as an apple is the fruit of natural life.

What should be our first step? It should be to come to the Lord in repentance and confession, admitting our coldness of heart, acknowledging our lack of concern for His glory and of longing after righteousness, and expressing faith in Him.

"Blessed are they which do hunger and thirst after righteousness: for they shall be filled" (Matthew 5:6). May the Lord give us a sensitivity to sin, to all that displeases Him. In this crucial day and generation, may the driving power of all of our lives, all that we do and all that we are, be a supreme and overwhelming love for God and a longing to see Him glorified, for His name's sake.

Chapter 3: **The Road Builder**

THROUGHOUT NORTH AMERICA the road builder is at work. With hundreds of different types of machinery and thousands of men, he is engaged in building new superhighways across the length and breadth of this continent.

Nothing is allowed to stand in the way of his huge earth-moving machines. Mountains are leveled, valleys are filled in, crooked roads are straightened, and rough areas are resurfaced and made smooth. In mountain areas and in desert lands the roadbuilder's work goes on.

This is precisely the process described by the prophet Isaiah:

. . . .
"In the wilderness prepare the way of the Lord,
   make straight in the desert a highway for our God.
Every valley shall be lifted up,
   and every mountain and hill be made low;
the uneven ground shall become level,
   and the rough places a plain."

(Isaiah 40:3, 4)

When I last visited some friends of mine in the town of Tetuan in Morocco, the street in which they lived

39

was dirty, uneven, and undrained. But in 1959 the King of Morocco paid a visit to the Basha who lives in that street, and in preparation for his coming the street was paved and drained; its smells vanished forever. This was common procedure in the days during which the Old Testament was written. A way was prepared for a king, his path was smoothed, and a road was constructed.

The preparation of the "highway for our God," the road in the desert, is taking place throughout all history. In this process God has used prophets and apostles, kings and peasants. It is impossible to see from one isolated group the over-all plan of the Master Architect; nevertheless the plan is there. No mountain range or valley is permitted to frustrate His plan and purpose. God makes even the wrath of man to praise Him (Psalm 76:10).

The Old Testament tells us that God has a program, a plan that concerns not merely one nation but every nation. We frequently base our missionary messages upon the New Testament, and it is sometimes easy to overlook the fact that from "before the foundation of the world" God had a plan for world evangelism.

The first clear indication of the wide scope of God's plan was given to Abraham:

Now the Lord said to Abram, "Go from your country and your kindred and your father's house to the land that I will show you. And I will make of you a great nation, and I will bless you, and make your name great, so that you will be a blessing. I will bless those who bless you, and him who curses you I will curse; and by you *all families of the earth will bless themselves*" (Genesis 12:1-3).

". . . by your descendants shall all the nations of the earth bless themselves, because you have obeyed my voice" (Genesis 22:18).

". . . Abraham shall become a great and mighty nation, and all the nations of the earth shall bless themselves by him" (Genesis 18:18).

When God called Abraham to an unknown destination, he was calling him to be the first, and in some ways the greatest, of the "road builders" in the Old Testament. The fact that he was ignorant of his destination is significant. He was called primarily not to a country but to a Person. The key to his life is not his geographic location, but his relationship with God and obedience to His will.

God revealed in the very beginning of the Old Testament that His purpose was eventually to reach "all families" and "all nations." This fact is stressed again and again in the book of the Psalms:

> All the ends of the earth shall remember
> and turn to the Lord;
> and all the families of the nations
> shall worship before him.
>
> (Psalm 22:27)

41

"Ask of me, and I will make the nations your heritage,
and the ends of the earth your possession."

(Psalm 2:8)

May God be gracious to us and bless us
and make his face to shine upon us,
that thy way may be known upon earth,
thy saving power among all nations.
Let the peoples praise thee, O God;
let all the peoples praise thee!

Let the nations be glad and sing for joy,
for thou dost judge the peoples with equity
and guide the nations upon earth.
Let the peoples praise thee, O God;
let all the peoples praise thee!

(Psalm 67:1-5)

The prophets make clear the fact that this blessing of
the nations will come through the promised Messiah:

Behold my servant, whom I uphold,
my chosen, in whom my soul delights;
I have put my spirit upon him,
he will bring forth justice to the nations.

(Isaiah 42:1)

. . . .

"It is too light a thing that you should be my servant,
to raise up the tribes of Jacob
and to restore the preserved of Israel;
I will give you as a light to the nations,
that my salvation may reach to the end of the earth."

(Isaiah 49:6)

42

Arise, shine; for your light has come,
    and the glory of the Lord has risen upon you.
For behold, darkness shall cover the earth,
    and thick darkness the peoples;
but the Lord will arise upon you,
    and his glory will be seen upon you.
And nations shall come to your light,
    and kings to the brightness of your rising.
                      (Isaiah 60:1-3)

As a prisoner of war, Daniel had the heartbreaking experience of being dragged away hundreds of miles to a foreign country. But for this man of God his experience was in no sense a defeat, but rather a much wider opportunity for ministry and witness. He became a missionary to four different kings and their courts—first to King Nebuchadnezzar of Babylon, then to his son, King Belshazzar, then to King Darius the Mede, and finally to Cyrus, king of Persia.

It was during the reign of Belshazzar that Daniel said,

I saw in the night visions,
and behold, with the clouds of heaven
    there came one like a son of man,
and he came to the Ancient of Days
    and was presented before him.
And to him was given dominion
    and glory and kingdom,
that all peoples, nations, and languages
    should serve him;
his dominion is an everlasting dominion,
    which shall not pass away,

43

and his kingdom one
that shall not be destroyed.
(Daniel 7:13-14)

Jonah was another Old Testament missionary, albeit a reluctant one. The book that bears his name gives us a fascinating insight into the purposes of God in a "foreign" nation.

The last voice that rings down the years to us from the Old Testament reiterates this message:

"For from the rising of the sun to its setting my name is great among the nations, and in every place incense is offered to my name, and a pure offering; for my name is great among the nations, says the Lord of hosts" (Malachi 1:11).

As we read the last promises of the Old Testament,

"But for you who fear my name the sun of righteousness shall rise, with healing in its wings . . . Behold, I will send you Elijah the prophet before the great and terrible day of the Lord comes. And he will turn the hearts of fathers to their children and the hearts of children to their fathers, lest I come and smite the land with a curse" (Malachi 4:2, 5).

How good to know that these promises were not merely for the small group of people who comprised the nation of Israel and Judah. Throughout the entire Old Testament God reiterated that these blessings are "for every nation."

The process was long and devious, the pattern hard

44

to follow at times, the men He used from many and varied backgrounds, but God was building His road. Some men were road builders because of what they were, and God used other men in this process despite what they were. But always the original objective was in view: "the glory of the Lord shall be revealed, and all flesh shall see it together . . ." (Isaiah 40:5). Within this plan of God there was room for men, men of all nations.

It seems amazing that after the death of Christ the disciples were so slow to see that God had a purpose for other nations in addition to their own. But it is in Paul, the "apostle to the Gentiles," that we have perhaps the finest summary of this purpose:

> Welcome one another, therefore, as Christ has welcomed you, for the glory of God. For I tell you that Christ became a servant to the circumcised to show God's truthfulness, in order to confirm the promises given to the patriarchs, and in order that the Gentiles might glorify God for his mercy. As it is written,
> "Therefore I will praise thee among the Gentiles,
>   and sing to thy name";
> and again it is said,
> "Rejoice, O Gentiles, with his people";
> and again,
> "Praise the Lord, all Gentiles, and let all the peoples praise him";
> and further Isaiah says,
> "The root of Jesse shall come, he who rises to rule the Gentiles; in him shall the Gentiles hope."

45

> May the God of hope fill you with all joy and peace in believing, so that by the power of the Holy Spirit you may abound in hope (Romans 15:7-13).

We, too, have a part in this road-building program and we look to the time when . . .

> Then the seventh angel blew his trumpet, and there were loud voices in heaven, saying, "The kingdom of the world has become the kingdom of our Lord and of his Christ, and he shall reign for ever and ever." And the twenty-four elders who sit on their thrones before God fell on their faces and worshiped God (Revelation 11:15, 16).

We have hardly touched the fringe of God's redemptive purposes for the world as revealed in the Old Testament, but at least we can see that from the beginning He planned to reach "all nations" and determined to do this through other men.

The Old Testament tells how He prepared a nation as the womb from which the Savior of the world was to be born, a culture that was to be the cradle of the Church.

As we pause to look back over the centuries of the long-maturing purpose of God, we marvel at His concern for the world and the fact that it has always been His way to use men to reach men, rejoicing that in this majestic enterprise we have a part to play.

Chapter 4: "Other Sheep I Have"

Suppose the only part of the New Testament we had were the four gospels. This is the position of many people in the world today. They have the gospels in their language but no Old Testament and not much else of the New Testament.

Would we see in these four books enough concerning world evangelism to make us realize that we have a responsibility to take the gospel to people throughout the entire world?

Probably the most frequently quoted text in the entire Bible is the sixteenth verse of the third chapter of the Gospel of John: "For God so loved the world that he gave his only Son, that whoever believes in him should not perish but have eternal life. For God sent the Son into the world, not to condemn the world, but that the world might be saved through him" (John 3:16, 17). At once we see that God is concerned with the whole world.

During his life Jesus Christ accepted certain limitations that were imposed by his having a human body. For instance, as God, in His preincarnate existence, He was by nature and attribute omnipresent. Yet, as a man,

47

He appeared in only one place at a time. Almost His entire ministry was devoted to the Jewish nation which resided within the boundaries of what we would call Palestine today. But it is clear that Jesus Christ was *ultimately* concerned with all nations: "And I have other sheep, that are not of this fold; I must bring them also, and they will heed my voice. So there shall be one flock, one shepherd" (John 10:16).

Even though the purpose of God *at that time* was being worked out through one nation and one people, the heart and mind of Jesus Christ was reaching out far beyond the geographic barriers of that country to others of different races and of different countries. This thought is developed in a different context and from a different perspective in Matthew 21:

"Hear another parable. There was a householder who planted a vineyard, and set a hedge around it, and dug a wine press in it, and built a tower, and let it out to tenants, and went into another country. When the season of fruit drew near, he sent his servants to the tenants, to get his fruit; and the tenants took his servants and beat one, killed another, and stoned another. Again he sent other servants, more than the first; and they did the same to them. Afterward he sent his son to them, saying 'They will respect my son.' But when the tenants saw the son, they said to themselves, 'This is the heir; come, let us kill him and have his inheritance.' And they took him and cast him out of the vineyard, and killed him. When therefore the owner of the vineyard comes, what will he do to those tenants?" They said to him, "He will put those wretches to a miserable death, and let out the vineyard to other tenants who will give him the fruits in their seasons."

Jesus said to them, "Have you never read in the scriptures:

'The very stone which the builders rejected
has become the head of the corner;
this was the Lord's doing,
and it is marvelous in our eyes'?

Therefore I tell you, the kingdom of God will be taken away from you and given to a nation producing the fruits of it." (Matthew 21:33-44).

These are terrible words so far as the Jewish people are concerned. At the same time they make a chink in the curtain that hides God's purposes and allow us to gain a glimpse of the tremendous scope of His plan of salvation. It is not for one isolated, ethnic group but for a limitless, spiritual nation that shall encompass every tongue and every people.

The clearest statement of this concern for the entire world occurs between Jesus' resurrection and His ascension to heaven. During this time Jesus held a number of interviews with His disciples, sometimes appearing to one individual, sometimes to two, and sometimes to large groups. (The record of this period is found in five different places in the New Testament: Matthew 28, Mark 16, Luke 24, John 20 and 21, Acts 1. These are exceedingly significant chapters and will repay a careful study. To study them in a harmony of the gospels is particularly helpful.)

49

In these various interviews, Jesus Christ did not attempt to refresh the minds of the disciples concerning all the truth He had already taught them. There were two truths He seemed determined to establish in their minds and He spared no pains to make it perfectly clear that they understood. The first truth: He had indeed risen from the dead. The second truth: They were to be witnesses of this fact throughout all the world.

It is interesting to see how Jesus Christ set about this and to follow the progress of thought in the various interviews. We shall deal with only three of them.

On the first day He had risen from the dead (Sunday evening):

> On the evening of that day, the first day of the week, the doors being shut where the disciples were, for fear of the Jews, Jesus came and stood among them and said to them, "Peace be with you." When he had said this, he showed them his hands and his side. Then the disciples were glad when they saw the Lord. Jesus said to them again, "Peace be with you. As the Father has sent me, even so I send you." And when he had said this, he breathed on them, and said to them, "Receive the Holy Spirit. If you forgive the sins of any, they are forgiven; if you retain the sins of any, they are retained" (John 20:19-23).

This is a rewarding passage to study, but we must content ourselves with the following observations. Why should Jesus Christ "show them His hands and His side"? The first truth that Jesus Christ wanted to establish was the fact that He had risen from the dead.

50

What better proof of identity than the wounds in the hands of the One who had so recently been crucified and the wound in the side where the spear of the centurion had so recently been planted? These wounds represented the very worst that men could do. When Jesus appeared to His disciples in this way, he not only proved to them that it was He himself but demonstrated that He had conquered the bonds of death.

If we had been looking for a group of men that could take a message and, by it, shake the world, we would hardly have looked twice at this group of fearful, puzzled, defeated men, gathered behind locked doors in this upper room. But the second truth that Jesus wanted to establish in their minds was that He was committing to them the most important assignment ever given to any group of men in the history of the world: "As the Father has sent me, even so I send you." As yet, the scope of this ministry is not defined, but its importance and grandeur are clearly indicated.

As J. H. Jowett points out:

> The "even so" which associates the two sentences on the same level of thought and purpose is majestic and divine. It places the mission of the Galilean fishermen in line with the redemptive mission of the Son of God. (*The Preacher, His Life and Work*, 5th ed., London, Hodder and Stoughton, p. 22.)

"As the Father has sent me." This phrase recalls the wonder of God's sending forth His Son from the riches of heaven to redeem mankind. Even the angels are

51

amazed at such a revelation of the love of God and the wisdom of God. Now, in the same breath as it were, Jesus Christ links His commission with that of His own disciples: "even so I send you."

For us to put these two ministries in the same breath would approach blasphemy, but Jesus does precisely this, lifting forever our service onto the highest possible plane. The call to world evangelism, as yet not too specific, is exciting in its wonder and privilege: "To me, though I am the very least of all the saints, this grace was given, to preach to the Gentiles the unsearchable riches of Christ" (Ephesians 3:8).

For the next post-resurrection interview we have to make a journey. On the morning that Jesus Christ rose from the dead, the angel informed the two women,

> "Then go quickly and tell his disciples that he has risen from the dead, and behold, he is going before you to Galilee; there you will see him" ... Then Jesus said to them, "Do not be afraid; go and tell my brethren to go to Galilee, and there they will see me" (Matthew 28:7, 10).

At the time these words were spoken the disciples were in Jerusalem. Moreover, it was in Jerusalem that they were eventually "to wait for the promise of the Father ... 'before many days you shall be baptized with the Holy Spirit'" (Acts 1:4, 5). Why, then, was it necessary in the period that intervened for them to make the long trip into Galilee?

That they did make such a trip is apparent from I

Corinthians 15:6. We are told that after Jesus Christ had risen from the dead "he appeared to more than five hundred brethren at one time." Now this could not have been in Jerusalem, for in Acts 1:15 we learn that "the company of persons was in all about a hundred and twenty."

So this appearance of Jesus Christ to over five hundred disciples at one time must have been in Galilee. We remember that Jesus Christ spent the greater part of His earthly life ministering in the area of Galilee and had many followers there. The two truths He so emphatically stressed to the disciples in Jerusalm had to be forcibly demonstrated also to the church that was in Galilee. In Matthew 28 we have the record of this appearance:

> Now the eleven disciples went to Galilee, to the mountain to which Jesus had directed them. And when they saw him they worshiped him; but some doubted. And Jesus came and said to them, "All authority in heaven and on earth has been given to me. Go therefore and make disciples of all nations, baptizing them in the name of the Father and of the Son and of the Holy Spirit, teaching them to observe all that I have commanded you; and lo, I am with you always, to the close of the age" (Matthew 28:16-20).

In this interview in Galilee the same two truths were expressed: First, Jesus Christ had risen from the dead. When they saw His appearance, some doubted, but most of them recognized Him as risen, victorious Lord and worshiped Him. And second, there was the truth of world evangelism: "'Go therefore and make disciples of all nations.'"

Note the carefulness with which Jesus Christ impressed these truths upon His disciples. In this particular interview, He was considerably more specific than in the previous one, both as to the scope of this commission, "all nations," and also as to the nature of it, "make disciples . . . baptizing . . . teaching them to observe all that I have commanded you."

And so the picture becomes clearer.

Following this interview, the disciples returned from Galilee to Jerusalem where the final interview was given:

> . . . until the day when he was taken up, after he had given commandment through the Holy Spirit to the apostles whom he had chosen. To them he presented himself alive after his passion by many proofs, appearing to them during forty days, and speaking of the kingdom of God. And while staying with them he charged them not to depart from Jerusalem, but to wait for the promise of the Father, which, he said, "you heard from me, for John baptized with water, but before many days you shall be baptized with the Holy Spirit."
>
> So when they had come together, they asked him, "Lord, will you at this time restore the kingdom to Israel?" He said to them, "It is not for you to know times or seasons which the Father has fixed by his own authority. But you shall receive power when the Holy Spirit has come upon you; and you shall be my

witnesses in Jerusalem and in all Judea and Samaria and to the end of the earth." And when he had said this, as they were looking on, he was lifted up, and a cloud took him out of their sight" (Acts 1:2-9).

Again the same two truths emerge in this last interview Jesus Christ had on earth: the first, the proof that He had risen from the dead; the second, His commission to His disciples to take this message "to the end of the earth."

Actually, there was also a third truth He seemed careful to establish in these interviews. This was the fact that, although He was giving to them a task to perform, He was also promising them a power with which to perform it.

When He said, "even so I send you" (John 20:21), He also "breathed on them, and said to them, 'Receive the Holy Spirit'" (John 20:22). When He said, "Go therefore and make disciples of all nations" (Matthew 28:19), He also said, "Lo, I am with you always, to the close of the age" (Matthew 28:20). When He said, "You shall be my witnesses . . . to the end of the earth" (Acts 1:8), He also said, "But you shall receive power when the Holy Spirit has come upon you" (Acts 1:8).

Martin Luther once said that we can easily be too big for God, but we can never be too small for Him. Certainly these men were small enough, so that when the Holy Spirit did begin to work through them it was obvious to all men that it was God at work. It is this truth that translates the commission from a burden to a privilege. Nothing is more exciting and stimulating than setting out to do the impossible with the Lord.

In the light of some of the things that we have seen in this chapter, it is almost incomprehensible that the very men to whom Jesus expressed himself most clearly and repeatedly were unable to see His interest in other people apart from their own Jewish nation. His concern was for the uttermost parts of the earth; His will was that the Gentiles as well as Jews should hear the Word of God.

Nevertheless, in Acts 11:1-3 we read, "Now the apostles and the brethren who were in Judea heard that the Gentiles also had received the word of God. So when Peter went up to Jerusalem, the circumcision party criticized him, saying, 'Why did you go to uncircumcised men and eat with them?' "

Lest we be too hard on the disciples, let us remember how slow we are to understand the wideness of God's love and the scope of His redemption.

> For the love of God is broader
>   Than the measures of man's mind;
> And the heart of the Eternal
>   Is most wonderfully kind.
>   F. W. Faber

As we have seen, the period of fifty odd days between the Crucifixion and Pentecost were of tremendous significance for the disciples and for us.

The fact that Jesus expected His followers to evangelize the world was stated as a command and was amplified and reiterated. It was given to a small group of leaders; it was proclaimed in the presence of over 500 people. The command was given in Jerusalem and repeated in Galilee. Of all the truths that Jesus could have taught in these days, this was *the* truth that He chose to burn into the minds of His followers.

There is no command in Scripture more explicitly stated or so frequently repeated. That this purpose is dear to the heart of the Savior is clear by the times that He refers to it in this crucial period.

To obey the Lord is mandatory. Further, obedience is evidence of our love for Him. "If you love me, you will keep my commandments." "He who has my commandments and keeps them, he it is who loves me" (John 14:15, 21). If we are making no contribution *at this time* to the evangelization of the world, we are living in the sin of disobedience, of unlove.

If as we prepare for our careers, we are giving little consideration to the fact that He may want us to serve overseas, or if we feel that our responsibility is small because we believe we are called to stay at home, we are out of tune with the heart of God and grieving Him with our indifference to His heart's desire.

Chapter 5: **From Jerusalem to the End of the Earth**

THE GROUP OF DISCIPLES on Mount Olivet is dispersing slowly, as if reluctant to leave the place where they saw their Lord for the last time. Ringing in their ears are phrases uttered by Jesus Christ that very day: ". . . you shall receive power . . . you shall be my witnesses"—and even stranger words of the angel, "This Jesus, who was taken up from you into heaven, will come in the same way as you saw him go into heaven" (Acts 1:8, 11).

Imagine the ponderings of the disciples as they walk from Mount Olivet back to Jerusalem. Witnesses of Jesus in Jerusalem? It is more than six weeks since He rose from the dead, and certainly they have made no impact on Jerusalem yet. Where will they start? How will they go about it? And then Jesus said something about Judea and Samaria and the end of the earth!

When we bear in mind the tremendous scope of this commission and the utter inadequacy of the men to whom He gave the task, it certainly seems hopeless. But Jesus did not cajole or coerce them to be witnesses. Rather He promised, "You shall receive power when the Holy Spirit has come upon you; and you shall *be* my witnesses . . ." (Acts 1:8). It is exciting to see later the difference in these men as a result of this power. How wonderfully their mission was fulfilled.

Jerusalem

"So those who received his (Peter's) word were baptized, and there were added that day about three thousand souls . . . And fear came upon every soul; and many wonders and signs were done through the apostles . . . praising God and having favor with all the people. And the Lord added to their number day by day those who were being saved" (Acts 2:41, 43, 47).

A tremendous impact was immediately made upon Jerusalem. The third, fourth and fifth chapters of the Acts of the Apostles reveal how great was the impression made upon those who lived in Jerusalem. For example, ". . . many of those who heard the word believed; and the number of the men came to about five thousand" (Acts 4:4).

The sick were healed, miracles were performed. Supernatural boldness and poise characterized these men as they witnessed to Jesus Christ. There was a wonderful unity of love and devotion on the part of the apostles and disciples, and "great grace was upon them all" (Acts 4:33). All the time the Lord was expanding the church in number as well as in quality. "None of the rest dared join them, but the people held them in high

59

honor. And more than ever believers were added to the Lord, multitudes both of men and women" (Acts 5:13, 14). There was no doubt about the way in which they witnessed in Jerusalem.

Judea

Judea was the country around Jerusalem.

"The people also gathered from the towns around Jerusalem, bringing the sick and those afflicted with unclean spirits, and they were all healed" (Acts 5:16). It is significant to note that the first spread of the gospel from Jerusalem into the towns and villages of Judea was not accomplished by evangelistic missions fanning out from Judea, but rather from the people of Judea coming into Jerusalem.

The Lord was doing such remarkable things in the city that, out of need and perhaps also curiosity, people were drawn from surrounding areas to observe and participate in the blessing that was shaking Jerusalem.

The next step in this process was a direct repercussion of the murder of Stephen. "And on that day a great persecution arose against the church in Jerusalem; and they were all scattered throughout the region of Judea and Samaria, except the apostles" (Acts 8:1).

So effective was the witness of the disciples to Jesus Christ in Jerusalem that there was a violent and sustained attempt to stamp out the Church by persecution. But Satan overreached himself.

60

A man who attempts to put out a campfire by scattering the ashes with his foot is apt to find that instead of extinguishing one blaze, he has kindled a dozen new ones. Everywhere that a live coal falls in dry grass, a new fire is kindled. So it happened with the spread of the gospel.

The attempt to destroy the Church by persecution succeeded only in scattering the believers. "Now those who were scattered went about preaching the word" (Acts 8:4). Thus the opposition of man and the enmity of Satan were turned to the glory of God.

Samaria

Samaria was the semi-foreign area in the north that separated Judea from Galilee. "And on that day a great persecution arose against the church in Jerusalem; and they were all scattered throughout the region of Judea and *Samaria*. . . . Now those who were scattered went about preaching the word. Philip went down to a city of Samaria, and proclaimed to them the Christ. And the multitudes with one accord gave heed to what was said by Philip, when they heard him and saw the signs which he did . . . Now when the apostles at Jerusalem heard that Samaria had received the word of God, they sent to them Peter and John . . . Now when they had testified and spoken the word of the Lord, they returned to Jerusalem, preaching the gospel to many villages of the Samaritans" (Acts 8:1, 4-6, 14, 25).

61

The whole eighth chapter of Acts is a stimulating record of the Lord's work, but there are two particularly significant things for us to observe now.

The first of these is the spontaneity of this whole evangelistic movement. It was about as carefully planned and premeditated as a prairie fire or a tidal wave!

The second remarkable thing to note is the people God used in this movement. We are expressly told, "They were all scattered . . . *except* the apostles" (Acts 8:1). Therefore, it was not the leaders of the church in Jerusalem who were carrying out this evangelism; it was the Spirit of God working through the rank and file.

It is interesting that modern theology is busily rediscovering the teaching of Scripture on "the ministry of the laity." The tragedy is that this aspect of the work of the Spirit through the Church of Christ was overlooked for centuries. And the great formal religions are not the sole offenders, with their tendency to rely on the ordained and the professionals. Every church and student group needs to recognize the fact that God's method is men, and God's men are often rather unlikely people, humanly speaking.

Surely within every group of believers, be it in a community or on a university campus, the Spirit of God is waiting to supply all that is needed for effective witness to Jesus Christ.

In the first eight chapters of the Acts of the Apostles,

we have seen that three out of the four areas of Christ's Commission were fulfilled—Jerusalem, Judea and Samaria. But what of the uttermost parts of the earth?

The Uttermost Parts of the Earth

Although in the early chapters of the Acts of the Apostles the spread of the gospel was dramatic, it was geographic and not cultural. It spread widely, but failed to burst the bonds of Jewish culture. "Now those who were scattered because of the persecution that arose over Stephen traveled as far as Phoenicia and Cyprus and Antioch, speaking the word to none except Jews" (Acts 11:19).

In Acts 10 we see the infinite pains that our Lord took with Peter to break down his cultural prejudice. When He said the gospel should be preached in "the uttermost parts," he meant not merely to Jews scattered in the uttermost parts, but also to natives of those areas. "But there were some of them, men of Cyprus and Cyrene, who on coming to Antioch spoke to the Greeks also, preaching the Lord Jesus. And the hand of the Lord was with them, and a great number that believed turned to the Lord" (Acts 11:20, 21).

As a stone thrown into the calm waters of a lake will produce an ever-widening circle of ripples, so this gospel spread. Geographically, it spread to Jerusalem, Judea, Samaria, Syria, Cyprus, and Phoenicia. Culturally, it

63

spread beyond the Jewish nation to Romans and to Greeks.

In embryo, the whole commission of Jesus Christ had been fulfilled by the eleventh chapter of the Acts of the Apostles—within a space of about five years. All that has taken place in the centuries since then has been only an extension of that work.

Certainly, the church in Jerusalem obeyed the Commission of Jesus Christ with such dramatic results that we are prompted to ask, "Why was it so successful?" "What kind of church was it that made it so effective?" "What were the characteristics of this successful church and how can we copy them?"

We find the clearest description of this church in Acts 2:42-47. Detailed exposition of this passage is beyond the scope of this book, but one or two of the distinctive characteristics of this church merit comment, for they are vital for us today:

1. ". . . they devoted themselves to the apostles' teaching" (v. 42). This certainly does not mean that they listened to sermons and commented favorably upon them, but that there was a wholehearted giving of themselves to the teaching of the apostles which became our New Testament.

Significantly, one of the first evidences of regeneration is that the Bible, previously "just another book," becomes vital and living. One of the evidences of the Holy Spirit in the life of an individual, or in a group of Christians, is vitality in Bible study and obedience to

64

the truths learned in Bible study. Often "the apostles' teaching" is present in the individual "quiet time," in pulpit preaching, and in group Bible studies; but there is little vitality with it. This certainly was not true of the church in Jerusalem.

2. ". . . they devoted themselves to . . . fellowship" (v. 42). We never discover fellowship by seeking it per se, but we stumble over it, as it were, on the pathway of obedience and service.

Whenever there is a movement of God in revival, one of the outcomes inevitably and immediately is a tremendous experience of fellowship with other believers that transcends all barriers of denomination and culture. Often we try to create fellowship ourselves and finish with an artificial counterfeit. If we lack either of these distinctive qualities of love for God's Word and His children, we should seek for the cause of their absence.

3. "And they devoted themselves to . . . prayers" (v. 42). As we read through the early chapters of the Acts of the Apostles, we see something of the tremendous effectiveness of Christians' praying. Prison doors were unlocked, people were healed, the disciples were made bold, the house where they were meeting was shaken.

It is a sad commentary on the church today that most prayer meetings are a bore. I doubt if you could have been in the church in Jerusalem and been bored in the prayer meeting!

65

Soon after I was ordained, I accepted the pastorate of a small church. One of the things that disturbed me about the church was the deadness of the prayer meeting. I tried every device that I could think of to bring some measure of life and vitality to it. I changed the night on which the prayer meeting was held; for a time I tried confining it only to the young people of the church; I had the people sit in rows, then in a circle; I suggested that they kneel, allowed them to sit, urged them to pray short prayers, experimented with different types of music. After a year and utterly beaten, I had to confess to the Lord that if ever this prayer meeting were to live, He would have to be the One to give it life.

That life did come, but it took a long time. Over a period of several years, as one and another of us were drawn closer to the Lord, there came a real breath of quickening. Without gadgets or gimmicks, vitality in the prayer meeting became pronounced. One man attended the prayer meeting for the first time and confessed to me after it was over: "When I came into this meeting, I had no sense of spiritual need whatsoever. But when I heard these people pray, I knew they had a spiritual experience that I did not possess." That evening he found Jesus Christ as his Savior.

The remedy is not to organize better prayer meetings. It is to recognize lack of spontaneity in praying as one of many evidences of lack of spiritual reality in our lives and in our groups.

4. "And fear came upon every soul; and many wonders and signs were done through the apostles" (v. 43). It is doubtful whether we should necessarily expect to see the wonders and the signs done through us that were done through the apostles, although it must be confessed that we are far more apt to expect too little than too much. What is clear, however, is that where the Spirit of the living God is dwelling in an individual or in a group, there ought to be some evidence of His presence and His power.

Counseling with a young lady, I asked her, "How long have you been a Christian?" She replied, "Fifteen years." I said, "What do you have as a Christian that the people with whom you work and come into contact do not have?" After a few moments of silence she replied, "Nothing."

It is easy for us to accept, and forget, the fact that we are "the temples of the Holy Ghost." But there is precious little evidence of any superhuman or supernatural power, either in our lives or in our service. Granted that spiritual power does not necessarily, or even normally, reveal itself in sensational or flashy ways, nevertheless there often is little or no evidence of the working of the Lord with us.

We expect nothing from God and get it every time.

5. "And the Lord added to their number day by day those who were being saved" (v. 47). God does not give all His children the same gifts. I do not believe He has given to every one of us the gift of soul-winning

67

and evangelism. But if there is one thing the Scripture teaches clearly, it is that every Christian is called to be a witness.

The criterion of spiritual success is not necessarily soul-winning. Many godly people have worked for many years among Muslims and seen few, if any, converts. This should not blind us, however, to the fact that in most situations where the Lord has planted a body of believers, it is His will to use these believers to bring others to a knowledge of the Lord and into fellowship with himself and with His Church. What we need is not necessarily more evangelistic activity, but more evangelistic power. We ought to ask ourselves whether we have such evangelistic power and, if not, why not.

The reason that these distinctive characteristics have been mentioned is not that we may work harder at producing them for ourselves. As with natural fruit, these are an evidence of life and a product of growth.

It is commonly said that prayer brings revival. But it may be more exact to say that revival brings prayer. When Peter preached his sermon, in the second chapter of Acts, the immediate response of his hearers was, "Brethren, what shall we do?" And the response: "Peter said to them, 'Repent and be baptized every one of you in the name of Jesus Christ for the forgiveness of your sins; and you shall receive the gift of the Holy Spirit'" (vs. 37, 38). The people who asked the question were non-Christians, but the reply given by Peter

68

is a reply that reminds us of the twin principles of every Christian grace and blessing: first, confession of sin; second, faith in Jesus Christ.

If we are conscious that these distinctive characteristics are absent in our life and witness, it is probably either an indication that we need more reality in confession of sin, or more faith and expectation from the Lord.

The key to the uttermost parts of the earth is always Jerusalem. The greatest need on the mission fields of the world is revival in the homeland. Today the distinction between "foreign mission field" and "homeland" which "sends the missionary" is fast disappearing. Insofar as the distinction bred a patronizing attitude from the giver to the receiver, the disappearance is all to the good.

Many countries that are so-called mission fields are as developed spiritually and culturally as the western lands; many have churches that have been indigenous for years. But it is common for a church to be indigenous and dead.

Our great need is not so much more missionaries, but more spiritual power; not more prayers, but more reality in our present prayers. Only then shall we see in our day and generation the fulfillment of the Commission of Jesus Christ.

Chapter 6: **Motivation for Missionary Service**

GOD IS CONCERNED not merely with what we do but with why we do it. It is easy to do the right thing for the wrong reason.

Why do I preach? Because I am paid to preach? That is materialism. Because I enjoy preaching? That is selfishness. In order to help my church or denomination? That is ecclesiasticism.

Do I preach to further the cause of the mission board or society with which I work? That is organizationalism. Do I preach because I am interested in people and want to help them? That is humanitarianism. Do I preach because Jesus Christ wants me to preach? That's Christianity.

But it is difficult to keep a real balance. Perhaps the greatest deficiency in the Reformation was the lack of missionary zeal and vision in the ministry of most of the reformers. Preoccupied as they were with the immense task of the Reformation in Europe, and living in an age of great ignorance of geography, they showed little concern for those in the far corners of the earth. It is pos-

70

sible to have a wonderfully high conception of God and to exhibit little concern for the needs of men.

During the 1880's there was a tremendous growth of missionary vision and energy. During that period many modern mission boards were started, and many new mission fields were entered. The slogan in those days was: "The Evangelization of the World in This Generation."

This emphasis upon man and the need of man has dangers also. Such thinking does produce a tremendous sense of urgency and is simple to convey to other Christians. But it is man-centered rather than God-centered. Sometimes it expresses more interest in counting converts than in establishing churches, is more concerned with decisions than with obedience.

A combination of motives exist for world evangelism. Neglect of any one may lead to imbalance. A high view of God that fails to inspire interest in man is apt to induce neglect of man or, at best, chilly service performed as a joyless duty. On the other hand, a view focused on man to the neglect of God leads to a downgrading of the Church, undue emphasis upon results, and general superficiality. Both views fall far short of the New Testament standard.

Love for Man

Concern for people in distress is not peculiarly a Christian characteristic. When an earthquake strikes Mo-

71

rocco or famine stalks through India, non-Christians as well as Christians rush to bring help to those in need. We would like to think that countries with a strong Christian influence would have more sensitive consciences in this respect. Certainly a Christian who is anything like Jesus Christ will reflect the love and concern that He had with those in sorrow or need. "When he saw the crowds, he had compassion for them, because they were harassed and helpless, like sheep without a shepherd. Then he said to his disciples, 'The harvest is plentiful, but the laborers are few; pray therefore the Lord of the harvest to send out laborers into his harvest' " (Matthew 9:36-38).

The King James Version translates as "moved with compassion" a word occurring only four times in the New Testament. It is a strong word, indeed, meaning deeply moved. It occurs again in Matthew 14:14, "As he went ashore he saw a great throng; and he had compassion on them, and healed their sick." Did you ever stand on a street in a busy city and watch the faces of the people as they hurry to and fro? Our Lord could never look upon such a sight without being deeply moved. He saw people like lost sheep—bewildered, harassed, helpless. They were scattered and lost and sick, and He was moved within himself.

> And a leper came to him beseeching him, and kneeling said to him, "If you will, you can make me clean." Moved with pity, he stretched out his hand and touched him, and said to him, "I will; be clean." And

72

immediately the leprosy left him, and he was made clean (Mark 1:40-42).

What would be our opinion of a neurosurgeon who, being informed of a child involved in a highway accident and in need of his surgical help to live, nonchalantly planned to go to the movies? This analogy is not so farfetched as it may seem. Approximately 1.5 billion of the world's 2.9 billion people are still waiting to hear about Jesus Christ for the first time. And Christians are almost completely indifferent to this tragedy. Metaphorically speaking, they are at the movies.

If we have any compassion, any sense of the utter hopelessness of people without Christ, any comprehension of the sheer bleakness of their future in this life, and even more the next, how can we live our lives with scarcely a thought of our responsibility to them?

Frederick Engel's account of the condition of the working class in England in the 1840's reveals the author as a man who, though inheriting a fortune and a prominent position in society, was deeply concerned with the appalling condition of so many people in the world. Although the Church has had her Wilberforces and her Shaftsburys, it is a sad commentary on her condition that she has often been less concerned about these injustices than the communists who exploit them for their own ends.

Any interest in the foreign field that lacks a true Christ-centered humanitarianism will lack urgency and it will lack compassion. To go to the mission field because of the need alone would be disastrous. But if we in our own comfort and safety can think of the human and eternal destiny of countless thousands throughout the world without facing the issue of our own responsibility, something is wrong with our spiritual life.

Obedience

As we have noted, the fifty days that intervened between the resurrection of Christ and His ascension were spent with two objects in view. The first was to convince the disciples of the fact of the resurrection and the second, to impress upon them the fact that they were being made responsible for taking this gospel to the uttermost parts of the earth.

No command in the Scripture is more specific or more often repeated than this. The Bible makes it clear that we cannot be indifferent to world evangelism and obedient to Jesus Christ. Further, we cannot be disobedient to Jesus Christ and love Him, for He tells us, "If you love me, you will keep my commandments" (John 14:15).

A phrase used in the ordination prayer when I was ordained to the ministry has remained in my memory: "Oh Lord, wilt thou ordain him with the pierced hand." Although the later years of my first pastorate were happy, the first few years were unhappy ones. There were times when nothing kept me in the ministry except the knowledge that I was there because

74

Christ had put me there, that my ordination had been not of man but of God. If we go out to meet the needs of people alone, only to find that they reject our ministry and are unappreciative of our efforts, the natural response will be to become disheartened and give up. When the way becomes difficult, obedience is the one motive for foreign missions that will keep us true to the Lord when all else would compel us to give up.

A Muslim in Arabia once said to Samuel Zwemer, "You have worked among us for years, you have seen no converts, you will see no converts; why do you stay?" To which Zwemer replied, "I am here because my Commander-in-Chief sent me here and I have to stay until His command is rescinded."

God certainly does not intend that everyone should go abroad as a foreign missionary. But it is evident from His Word that He has a program for world evangelism. If we are not playing an active role in this program in one way or another, at home or abroad, we are sinning against the Lord in disobedience.

Concern for God's Glory

"Now while Paul was waiting for them at Athens, his spirit was provoked within him as he saw that the city was full of idols" (Acts 17:16). History tells us that the Athens of Paul's day was not only an exceedingly cultured and educated city, but also a very idolatrous one. Every street had its quota of shrines, temples, and idols. According to one historian, "It was easier to find a god in Athens than it was to find a man."

When Paul observed this, he was provoked. He was deeply moved, though less with pity than with anger. His concern for the honor and the glory of God roused within him a deep sense of indignation and a longing to see his Lord vindicated and enthroned in this idolatrous place. For the Apostle Paul, this sense of indignation and provocation led to immediate action: "So he argued in the synagogue with the Jews and the devout persons, and in the market place every day with those who chanced to be there" (Acts 17:17).

This motivation for foreign missions—jealous concern for God's glory—is heard in the cry of the Psalmist:

Declare his glory among the nations,
    his marvelous works among all the peoples!
For great is the Lord, and greatly to be praised;
    he is to be feared above all gods.
For all the gods of the peoples are idols;
    but the Lord made the heavens.
Honor and majesty are before him;
    strength and beauty are in his sanctuary.

Ascribe to the Lord, O families of the peoples,
    ascribe to the Lord glory and strength!
Ascribe to the Lord the glory due his name;
    bring an offering, and come into his courts!
Worship the Lord in holy array;
    tremble before him, all the earth!

Say among the nations, "The Lord reigns! . . ."
                                    (Psalm 96:3-10)

I once visited the town of Kairouan in Tunisia and was shown the Grand Mosque. The town was built as a springboard for Arab attacks during the time when they subjugated North Africa. The mosque is built very largely from stones and pillars torn from Christian churches that the Muslims destroyed as they swept in. Halfway up the steps of the minaret, my attention was drawn to step which bore the outline of a fish.

In the early days of the Church of Jesus Christ, when a man wanted to be known as a Christian, he would have the sign of the fish painted or engraved in his home or place of business. In Greek, it represents an acrostic for the word "fish"—Jesus (the) Christ of God (the) Son (our) Savior. I have seen exactly the same sign in other Christian ruins throughout North Africa as well as in the catacombs in Rome.

What, then, was this sign doing in the steps of a Muslim minaret?

For thirteen centuries, as the Muezzin has climbed the steps of the minaret to call the faithful Muslims to prayer, he has stamped under foot the symbol of Jesus Christ and of His Lordship. He glories in the fact that it was in North Africa that the Church, once so strong that it numbered well over five hundred bishops, sustained its greatest defeat at the hands of the Muslims. There came into my heart that day a tremendous longing to see the name of Jesus Christ vindicated. We know that He is Lord, but millions throughout the world are still waiting to hear that fact declared.

77

O the joy to see Thee reigning,
Thee, my own beloved Lord!
    Every tongue Thy Name confessing,
    Worship, honor, glory, blessing
Brought to Thee with glad accord;
Thee, my Master and my Friend,
    Vindicated and enthroned;
Unto earth's remotest end
    Glorified, adored, and owned.

Frances R. Havergal

The Fear of God

"For we must all appear before the judgment seat of Christ, so that each one may receive good or evil, according to what he has done in the body. Therefore, knowing the fear of the Lord, we persuade men" (II Corinthians 5:10, 11).

There was a time in my life, during a period of spiritual declension, when I spent all my spare time debating and preaching politics. The gift the Lord had given for preaching was being used solely to influence men politically. It was then that the Lord spoke to me through the parable of the talents: "Every one to whom much is given, of him will much be required" (Luke 12:48). I had no illusions that I was a Charles Haddon Spurgeon or a Billy Graham, but I did know that God had given me some ability to speak and that some day I should have to account for the way I had discharged my stewardship and kept my trust.

78

". . . it is required of stewards that they be found trustworthy" (I Corinthians 4:2). Unquestionably, the Apostle Paul realized that one factor in his laboring was the knowledge that some day he would have to face the Lord at the judgment seat and account for the stewardship of his time, his energy, his gifts and his talents.

> . . . each man's work will become manifest; for the Day will disclose it, because it will be revealed with fire, and the fire will test what sort of work each one has done. If the work which any man has built on the foundation survives, he will receive a reward. If any man's work is burned up, he will suffer loss, though he himself will be saved, but only as through fire (I Corinthians 3:13-15).

How obvious it is that the Apostle Paul worked as one who would account for his work. Today fear is thought to be a meager motive, and *fear alone is* a meager motive. But to ignore God's opinion of our life and work is not trust; it is doubt of the judgment of God.

If we have received no gift nor talent other than the gift of the Gospel itself, we shall still have to account for the way that we guard this gift and pass it on to others. To enjoy so much when others have nothing will certainly be difficult to explain in eternity.

The Love of God

It would be dangerous to decree what should be the dominant influence in our motivation, but the love for God will certainly underlie all those factors that have been mentioned.

". . . the love of Christ controls us," says Paul (II Corinthians 5:14). Greatly gifted though he was in intellect, natural leadership, and ability, it was his flaming heart of love for Christ that drove him from country to country through suffering, persecution, privation, and shipwreck, making him the missionary that he was.

It is easy to sing about our love for Christ and profitable to do so; but if our love for Christ does not lead us to compassion for His children and for the lost, it is sentiment, not love.

The Love of His Appearing

Eschatology deals with the last things. It includes the study of doctrines relating to the second coming of Christ and the setting up of His kingdom. All the truths considered in this chapter should be accentuated by the truth of Christ's coming again.

It is significant that in Acts 1, the very passage of Scripture that says ". . . you shall be my witnesses in Jerusalem and in all Judea and Samaria and to the end of the earth," there is also the phrase, "Men of Galilee, why do you stand looking into heaven? This Jesus, who was taken up from you into heaven, will come in the same way as you saw him go into heaven" (Acts 1:8, 11).

We are not concerned here with the details of eschatology, about which there is a good deal of room for difference between sincere, dedicated Christians, but we are concerned that "this gospel of the kingdom will be preached throughout the whole world, as a testimony to all nations; and then the end will come" (Matthew 24:14).

The fact that our Lord is going to return, and that the end is going to come, accentuates another fact: the time is short for those who have as yet not heard about Jesus Christ. The time is short for us to reveal His glory. The time is short for us to obey His command. The time is short before we meet the Lord at the judgment seat to account for our stewardship.

We do not want to be missionary fanatics. Foreign missions is not the supreme truth; it is one of many important truths. But it is an *indispensable* truth.

It is not merely the responsibility of those who go abroad. Neither is it the hobby of a few enthusiasts, nor yet an optional extra. This is *the* mission of the Church of Jesus. Unless, by our service, by our praying, by our giving, and by our living we are fulfilling the Great Commission in our Jerusalem and to the uttermost parts of the earth, we are grieving the Holy Spirit of God by disobeying the command of Jesus Christ.

81

Chapter 7: **Missions and Prayer**

Why are missionaries so dependent upon people in the homeland?

We are constantly being told by missionary speakers that the missionary on the field depends on us, on our praying and on our giving.

Why has God made missionaries so dependent?

God could easily have provided for their financial needs apart from the somewhat vacillating generosity of donors in the homeland. And God could grant to them His power irrespective of whether or not people at home prayed for them. But God did choose to make them dependent, and there are three main reasons why this is so:

1. This is always God's way of working.

For just as the body is one and has many members, and all the members of the body, though many, are one body, so it is with Christ. For by one Spirit we were all baptized into one body—Jews or Greeks, slaves or free—and all were made to drink of one Spirit.

For the body does not consist of one member but of many. If the foot should say, "Because I am not a hand, I do not belong to the body," that would not make it any less a part of the body. And if the ear should say, "Because I am not an eye, I do not belong to the body," that would not make it any less a part of the body. If the whole body were an eye, where would be the hearing? If the whole body were an ear, where would be the sense of smell? . . . The eye cannot say to the hand, "I have no need of you," nor again the head to the feet, "I have no need of you" . . . If one member suffers, all suffer together; if one member is honored, all rejoice together.

Now you are the body of Christ and individually members of it (I Corinthians 12:12-27).

God has ordained that each member of His church should be dependent upon other members, just as each part of the body is dependent upon other parts of the body. He does not intend that any one of us should operate independently. Each of us is related to other members of the body of Christ.

2. The missionaries need it. Supposing God did supply the need of the missionary for money and prayer without reference to us. Imagine him setting out from home and loved ones and being swallowed up by the mists of distance. How forlorn and lonely would be his lot! The Scripture tells us that "God setteth the solitary in families . . ." (Psalm 68:6). It is part of the grace of God that He has given us this intimate and beautiful link between those who are serving on the foreign field and those who are behind.

3. The Christians at home need it. Anything that inspires me to give to the Lord is a blessing *to me*. Any-

thing that inspires me to pray is a blessing *to me*. The person who benefits most by the missionary's dependence is the person at home. This support is not merely a "spiritual chore"; it is a means of blessing and of grace.

There is so much that could be said on the subject of prayer, but we must limit ourselves to considering one or two basic facts which seem to be rather commonly overlooked. First of all, we shall look at the importance, then at the difficulties, of effective praying.

The Importance of Prayer

Whether we take Jesus Christ or the Apostle Paul as the example of the missionary par excellence, it is obvious that in their thinking and behavior prayer played a prominent part.

Paul had a particularly successful visit to Thessalonica. In his first letter to the young church there, he gave some hint of how important prayer was in his ministry by stating that he was "praying earnestly night and day that we may see you face to face and supply what is lacking in your faith" (I Thessalonians 3:10).

But it wasn't enough that he prayed for those among whom he ministered. In turn, he expected them to pray for his ministry that it might be prospered among others. For, later on in that same letter, he said, "Brethren, pray for us" (I Thessalonians 5:25). Still later he wrote, "Finally, brethren, pray for us, that the word

84

of the Lord may speed on and triumph, as it did among you, and that we may be delivered from wicked and evil men; for not all have faith" (II Thessalonians 3:1, 2).

He expressed somewhat similar thoughts when he wrote to the Colossians:

> Continue steadfastly in prayer, being watchful in it with thanksgiving; and pray for us also, that God may open to us a door for the word, to declare the mystery of Christ, on account of which I am in prison, that I may make it clear, as I ought to speak (Colossians 4:2-4).

There are innumerable instances in the life of Christ that illustrate the importance of prayer in our Lord's ministry, but we will look at just one illustration. It is found in the first chapter of the Gospel according to Mark. It is important that you look up this particular chapter in your Bible and read verses 21 through to the end of the chapter, verse 45.

These verses give us the account of a very busy day in Capernaum. On this particular Saturday morning Jesus preached in the synagogue. There He found himself in conflict with Satan in a case of demon possession. Jesus delivered the demoniac and cast out the spirit. This inevitably involved Him in more discussion and teaching. From verse 29 on, we read that immediately upon leaving the synagogue he entered the house of Simon, only to be confronted with another crisis, for Simon Peter's mother-in-law lay sick of a fever. Jesus

85

Christ immediately took charge of the situation and healed her fever. Verses 32 on tell us that in the evening "the whole city was gathered together about the door" (v. 33). What a crowd it was. ". . . all who were sick or possessed with demons . . . And he healed many who were sick with various diseases, and cast out many demons . . ." (vs. 32, 34). Other passages of the Gospels make clear to us that this healing ministry of Jesus Christ was costly, draining His energy.

This was the pattern, then, of that Saturday—long, crowded hours, with no seclusion or respite. And yet ". . . in the morning, a great while before day, he rose and went out to a lonely place, and there he prayed" (v. 35). The great lesson for us here is that, for Jesus Christ, prayer was more important than sleep.

It is easy to be extravagant in making the application of a verse like this. If, consistently and daily, we neglect our sleep to pray, it is almost inevitable that we will arrive at a state of physical and nervous exhaustion that will completely fail to bring glory to the Lord through our personal testimony and life. But it is utterly basic that we must absorb the *principle* that prayer is as indispensable as sleep.

But there is another lesson in this passage that is at once more important, more difficult, and less often discerned.

And Simon and those who were with him followed him, and they found him and said to him, "Every one is searching for you" (vs. 36, 37).

86

In other words, it was dark when Jesus departed to the lonely place to pray. With the dawn came the crowd, pressing once again with all its clamor, all its need. Simon and the other disciples followed Jesus to the lonely place (they evidently knew from practice where to find Him). We can almost detect a note of gentle reproach in the tone of Simon, "Lord, back in the village there's all the crowd, with their need of your teaching, with their sick to be healed. You are out here alone when all men are seeking you." To me, the reply of Jesus Christ is the most striking phrase in the whole of this chapter:

And he said to them, "Let us go on to the next towns, that I may preach there also; for that is why I came out" (vs. 38).

He didn't hurry back to the crowd; He knew He had pressing engagements ahead. With His time in the town of Capernaum so limited that He could not possibly meet all needs, He deliberately chose to spend in prayer time He could have spent healing the sick and teaching the truth. Thus we see the principle, not merely that prayer is more important than sleep but, what most of us find far more difficult to learn, that prayer is more important than work, even God's work. How tragic that so often the clamoring needs of men and the demands of Christian service are the very things that keep us from the lonely place.

But few of us enjoy praying. Many of us find it dif-

87

ficult to bring ourselves to pray. We find it all too easy
to stop praying once we start. Isn't it strange that anything that is so good for us and so pleasing to God
should be difficult for those who love the Lord?

There are many reasons to account for this. We must
certainly reckon with the attempt of Satan to frustrate
what is so obvious a hindrance to his nefarious plans.
But we should not blame it all on Satan. There are
other factors also. We turn now to consider three aspects of prayer which, if not rightly grasped, can lead
us into real difficulty and bondage, disarming us as far
as spiritual effectiveness is concerned.

God gives differing gifts to different individuals. I
have read the biographies of great men of prayer and
been rebuked again and again: by George Mueller, who
in answer to prayer received millions of dollars for his
orphan homes; by Hudson Taylor, of whom it was written, "The sun never rose in China but that it found
Hudson Taylor on his knees"; by Praying Hyde, so
called because of a ministry in prayer that changed the
lives of thousands in India and elsewhere.

Such biographies have been a blessing to thousands
of people. Yet I wonder if at times they have not been
a stumbling block also. To be stimulated by the example
of these men is beneficial, but to slavishly imitate them,
assuming that God's pattern for Hudson Taylor is God's
pattern for me, is completely to lose sight of the fact
that God deals with each one of us as individuals. What

is God's will for one man is not necessarily God's will for me.

A few years ago I was particularly stirred by reading the biography of Henry Frost of the China Inland Mission. An especially challenging fact was that his prayers were so much more specific than mine. He prayed for a certain sum of money; it was given. He prayed for a certain number of missionaries; they came. Encouraged by his example, and after spending a great deal of time in prayer and feeling that I knew the mind of the Lord, I prayed for a certain sum of money to be given to the mission with which I was then working, and had complete confidence that it would be forthcoming. Imagine my chagrin when the money did not come and when the prayer was not answered. There are blessings, however, in unanswered prayer, and the blessing in this prayer was that it drove me to consider this whole matter of a prayer ministry.

One conclusion to which I came was simply this, that just as God gave some men a very special ministry in preaching, so He gave other men a very special ministry in praying. This evidently was true of the giants of prayer who are mentioned in the previous paragraph. Paul tells us:

Now there are varieties of gifts, but the same Spirit; and there are varieties of service, but the same Lord; and there are varieties of working, but it is the same God who inspires them all in every one. To each is given the manifestation of the Spirit for the common good. To one is given through the Spirit the utterance of wisdom, and to another the utterance of knowledge according to the same Spirit, to another faith by the same Spirit . . . (I Corinthians 12:4-9).

It would seem that over and above our "saving faith" there is a specific "gift of faith," given to some who see answers to prayer that perhaps other Christians seldom see.

Paul summarizes this chapter in the last four verses, explaining that God has appointed many different gifts in the church. Then he adds:

Are all apostles? Are all prophets? Are all teachers? Do all work miracles? (I Corinthians 12:29).

By the same logic, we may ask ourselves, "Do all have the same gift of faith?" So far as I can discern, God has given to me certain spiritual gifts, but so far it does not seem to have been His will to give to me "the gift of faith" in the sense that it seems to be mentioned here and in the way that it was demonstrated in the life, for example, of George Mueller. This is not to say that I should not pray. But it is to say that it is very dangerous for me to assume that what George Mueller experienced I should experience, and that the pattern for his prayer life is the correct pattern for my prayer life.

A final word concerning this spiritual gift of faith. Paul urges us, "But earnestly desire the higher gifts" (I Corinthians 12:31). And perhaps the first thing for some of us to do, in terms of a missionary ministry, is to earnestly desire the gift of faith, to ask the Lord to give us the kind of insight and faith that will help us, by prayer, to accomplish untold victories in lands that perhaps we shall never visit.

The second fact that we often fail to recognize is that *there is variety in prayer.* Prayer has six forms. When we fail to recognize this, it leads to imbalance in our prayer life which, in turn, leads to frequent barrenness and frustration.

On an Algerian airfield on which I was stationed during the Second World War there was an Arab whose name was Giddimus. To be sure, his parents did not so name him; but so he was known to the hundreds of airmen with whom he came into contact. His knowledge of English was, to say the least, severely limited, and the phrase "giddi-mus" was the nearest that he could get to saying, "Give me . . ." But how he worked that phrase! "Giddi-mus cigarette, Johnny," "Giddi-mus candy, Joe," "Giddi-mus clothing," and thus, inevitably, he came to be known as "Giddimus."

All too many Christians have a "giddi-mus" mentality so far as prayer is concerned. Their only concept of prayer is ask, ask, ask from God.

What are the various forms of prayer? There are six different forms of prayer, and each one is important.

1. *Thanksgiving*

The place that thanksgiving occupies in the Psalms and in the writings of Paul attests to its importance in

91

the sight of God. ". . . give thanks in all circumstances; for this is the will of God in Christ Jesus for you" (I Thessalonians 5:18). ". . . always and for everything giving thanks in the name of our Lord Jesus Christ to God the Father" (Ephesians 5:20). "And let them offer sacrifices of thanksgiving, and tell of his deeds in songs of joy!" (Psalm 107:22). "He who brings thanksgiving as his sacrifice honors me" (Psalm 50:23).

It is obvious that no day's prayer time is complete without a period of thanksgiving. The basis of any healthy relationship should be appreciation. This is true of our relationship with God, thanksgiving being the expression of our appreciation and gratitude.

Such giving of thanks is not merely pleasing to God, it is indispensable to us. We seldom sing the old hymn today, but it does contain a very necessary truth:

When upon life's billows you are tempest-tossed,
When you are discouraged, thinking all is lost,
Count your many blessings, name them one by one,
And it will surprise you what the Lord has done.

Are you ever burdened with a load of care?
Does the cross seem heavy you are called to bear?
Count your many blessings, ev'ry doubt will fly,
And you will be singing as the days go by.

When you look at others with their lands and gold,
Think that Christ has promised you His wealth untold;
Count your many blessings, money cannot buy
Your reward in heaven, nor your home on high.

So, amid the conflict, whether great or small,
Do not be discouraged, God is over all;
Count your many blessings, angels will attend,
Help and comfort give you to your journey's end.
                              —*Johnson Oatman*

2. Praise

Many people confuse praise with thanksgiving.
Thanksgiving is mainly concerned with what God
gives, praise with what He is.

The main difference between the attitude of a man
toward his housekeeper and his wife is that, although
he will appreciate the help he gets from both, he will
love his wife for what she is. A wife does not merely
want to be appreciated for what she does, she wants to
be loved because of who she is. In praise and adoration
we express to God our love and our affection. ". . . the
true worshipers will worship the Father in spirit and
truth, for such the Father seeks to worship him" (John
4:23). When the Church was born in the outpouring
of the Holy Spirit at Pentecost, one of her first occupa-
tions was the exercise of praise and worship. ". . . we
hear them telling in our own tongues the mighty works
of God" (Acts 2:11). They "attending the temple together and breaking bread in their homes . . . partook
of food with glad and generous hearts, *praising God*
and having favor with all the people" (Acts 2:46, 47).

This is a greatly neglected form of prayer—probably
because it is so difficult to express ourselves concerning

the glory of God. You may find it helpful to make a list in the back of your Bible of suitable Psalms for use in the praise and worship of God, and read one (preferably aloud) each day in your Quiet Time. Here are some suggestions of Psalms to be used in this way: Psalm 66, 67, 86, 93, 95, 96, 97, 98, 99, 103, 111, 113, 146, 148, 149, 150. Hymns of praise and worship are a wonderful aid to praising the Lord, whether we read them quietly, quote them aloud, or sing them. Inter-Varsity's Hymns, "anywhere" Songs, and Christian Praise contain many such hymns.

The exercise of praise and adoration is God's will for us, but it also turns our attention away from ourselves and from our circumstances—the very best antidote for self-pity and depression.

3. Penitence

Attention focused in praise on the glory and holiness of God leads to a sense of our own unworthiness. When Isaiah "saw the Lord . . . high and lifted up," his response was "Woe is me! For I am lost; for I am a man of unclean lips" (Isaiah 6:1, 5).

Great men of God owe their godliness, not to sinlessness, but to their sensitivity to sin and their thorough repentance for sin.

Probably the most complete prayer of penitence is Psalm 51. Penitence is indispensable to close fellowship with the Lord and has three aspects: (a) self-examination (which was greatly stressed by the Puritans); (b) confession and repentance; and (c) the enjoyment of forgiveness. The enjoyment of forgiveness by faith keeps us from a morbid introspection and preoccupation with our sin.

The purpose of repentance is not to fill our minds with our sins, our failures, or ourselves. It is to put sin away that all our attention may be focused upon Jesus Christ.

4. Petition

Webster's Collegiate Dictionary defines the verb petition as "ask formally or earnestly." When we use the noun in connection with prayer, we refer to that part of prayer that is concerned with asking God for things that we need for ourselves. In a healthy prayer life, this will concern itself more with spiritual needs than with material needs. Recall our Lord's prayer in Matthew 6, where there is only one petition for material things (daily bread) compared with three requests for spiritual blessing and three requests concerning the kingdom and glory of God.

5. Intercession

In petition we pray for ourselves. In intercession we pray for others.

As Christians we need no human priest for we are all priests. "But you are a chosen race, a royal priesthood" (I Peter 2:9) to Him ". . . who loves us and has freed us from our sins by his blood and made us a kingdom,

95

priests to his God and Father . . ." (Revelation 1:5, 6). As priests it is our privilege and also our duty to pray for others.

This is the aspect of prayer that has a most direct and practical application to the mission field. In the life of every individual, in every student group, and in every church there should be a vital place given to intercessory prayer for those on the mission field. This will mean gathering information and taking an intelligent interest in a few missionaries and their situation. It will entail a sense of responsibility for entering into spiritual warfare by their sides, even though thousands of miles may separate us from them.

6. *Meditation*

The first five forms of prayer mentioned are all concerned with my speaking to God. But prayer is a two-way communion with God, and meditation on the Scripture is that form of prayer in which God speaks to me. It is important to realize that listening to God through the Word of God written is in itself a form of prayer.

For many of us it will occupy more of our time than any other form of prayer, and for some of us it may occupy more time than all the other forms of prayer.

If we approach the Bible as a textbook, the element of prayer will be absent. We must approach it as what it is, the Word of God, expecting Him to speak through it and being prepared to obey it in every detail. If God is not speaking to us through His Word, it is almost certainly an indication that somehow we have become estranged from Him.

If our prayer life is to be effective, we dare not neglect any one of these forms of prayer, but should make room for them every day.

Conditions for Effective Prayer

The Bible makes staggering promises about prayer, and Christians love to quote them. The Bible also establishes important conditions concerning prayer, but these are very rarely quoted.

We may focus our attention on a promise such as the one found in John 15, verse 7: "Ask whatever you will, and it shall be done for you." That is a wonderful promise indeed, and it is apparently unconditional; but if we stop to examine the context and consider other passages on prayer, we shall see that it is not unconditional at all. It is subject to strict conditions. The New Testament teaches that there are at least six conditions to be met before prayer can be effective.

1. *Faith*

". . . let him ask in faith, with no doubting, for he who doubts is like a wave of the sea that is driven and tossed by the wind" (James 1:6).

I once lived in a dormitory with a group of men who could not be trusted; personal belongings were stolen,

97

nothing much was safe. The resultant lack of mutual trust bred tension and misunderstanding, for where there is distrust between individuals, there can be no real harmony in personal relationships. In like manner, faith is basic to our harmonious relationship with God.

There is another reason why faith is basic to effective prayer: God's integrity is involved. As Hudson Taylor learned, and many learned through him, faith is really a resting of ourselves upon the faithfulness of God.

God could act without faith on our part, but He has chosen to make our whole prayer life, and indeed our whole Christian life, dependent upon our faith.

How do we increase our faith?

We do not increase our faith by singing a particular type of music or by attempting to "work it up." Faith is not a feeling. Faith is less concerned with the emotions than it is with the intellect and the will. But first of all, faith is a gift from God (Ephesians 2:8), and we begin by asking God to increase our faith.

Then we strengthen our faith by concentrating on the Word of God. "So faith comes from what is heard, and what is heard comes by the preaching of Christ" (Romans 10:17). As we focus our attention upon God through His Word, we see more of His power and glory, and our own confidence in Him is increased.

Faith is like a muscle: the more use it, the stronger it becomes.

Much of the ineffectiveness of our Christian life, and particularly of our prayer life, comes through unbelief.

". . . for whatever does not proceed from faith is sin" (Romans 14:23). We must be honest about our lack of faith and confess it to the Lord as sin.

2. *The right motive*

We read in James, chapter 4, verse 3: "You ask and do not receive, because you ask wrongly, to spend it on your passions." Even when we ask for the right thing we sometimes ask for the wrong reason. As we look at the prayer life of our Lord and of the Apostle Paul, we see that interest in their own well-being is eclipsed by concern for the glory of God and the success of His kingdom.

How important it is to be sure when we pray for anything that our prayer is dictated by the right motive, and not merely the desire to fulfill our own pleasures.

3. *The knowledge of God's will*

"And this is the confidence which we have in him, that if we ask anything *according to his will* he hears us" (I John 5:14). The standard of this verse accounts for the why of many unanswered prayers: they are not prayed with a knowledge of the will of God and in accord with the will of God.

To pray in the name of Jesus Christ is certainly to pray according to the will of God (John 14:13). But we must understand what that familiar term means. It does not mean a pagan-like reciting of "in Jesus' name" as though this phrase were a passkey to the Father's

99

hearing. It does not mean wrapping up our prayer requests by waving the name of Jesus over them like a magic wand. If we pray in Jesus' name, we shall ask only for things which are consistent with His name and for the glory of His name. We shall ask in Christ's stead—out of union with Him and out of a life that is pleasing to Him.

We read ". . . for we do not know how to pray as we ought . . ." (Romans 8:26). This and other passages of Scripture make clear that unless there is real fellowship with the Lord and an operation of the Holy Spirit in our minds and hearts, we are unable to fulfill this third condition of effective prayer because we are unable to pray according to His will.

How can we know His will?

This brings us to the next condition of effective prayer. We are beginning to see that each one of these conditions is directly related to the others.

4. *Abiding in Christ*

"If you abide in me, and my words abide in you, ask whatever you will, and it shall be done for you" (John 15:7). This promise is perhaps the most frequently quoted of all the New Testament promises concerning prayer. "Ask whatever you will, and it shall be done for you"—but as we look at the whole verse it is perfectly evident that this is not an unconditional promise. Verse and promise hinge upon those first few words, "*If* you abide in me."

100

How can we know the will of God? By abiding in Jesus Christ. If we are not living close to Him we cannot know His will. If we do not know His will, we cannot pray with the right motive. If we do not know His will, we cannot pray the prayer of faith. Most of us have no problems in believing that God can answer any prayer. Our problem is to know whether it is His will to answer a particular prayer. This we cannot know unless we are living with Him intimately enough to know His will.

"If you abide in me . . ." It is very clear that basically effective prayer depends upon our abiding relationship with Jesus Christ. How close God intends this abiding relationship to be is seen in the passage of John 15 from which that verse is taken. It is linked with the association of the vine with the branches. Jesus Christ says that just as the branches abide in the vine, so must we abide in Him. Only then can we know truly effective prayer.

This raises yet another question in our minds: How can we abide in Jesus Christ? Again we see the answer in still another condition of prayer.

5. *A pure heart*

Two sheets of ground glass will adhere together unless there is grit between them. The smallest piece of grit will serve to prevent the adhesion. So the smallest sin will prevent us from truly abiding in Christ and having intimacy of fellowship with Him.

101

Who shall ascend the hill of the Lord?
And who shall stand in his holy place?
He who has clean hands and a pure heart,
    who does not lift up his soul to what is false,
    and does not swear deceitfully.
(Psalm 24:3, 4)

If I had cherished iniquity in my heart,
    the Lord would not have listened.
(Psalm 66:18)

God's Word declares that the only basis on which a man can have fellowship with God is on the basis of holiness. God cannot commune with those whose "iniquities have separated between you and your God."

One of the most wonderful passages in the Scripture concerning abiding in Christ and walking in fellowship with Him occurs in the beginning of John's first letter: "If we walk in the light, as he is in the light, we have fellowship with one another, and the blood of Jesus his Son cleanses us from all sin. If we say we have no sin, we deceive ourselves, and the truth is not in us. If we confess our sins, he is faithful and just, and will forgive our sins and cleanse us from all unrighteousness" (I John 1:7-9).

Walking in fellowship with the Lord, abiding in Jesus Christ—this does not depend upon our never sinning; but it does depend upon our sensitivity to sin and immediate confession of sin. This kind of relationship necessitates "the blood of Jesus Christ cleansing us from

102

all sin," which in turn requires our recognition of sin and our readiness to confess our sin.

Unconfessed sin in the life of a believer will inevitably ruin his prayer life.

There is one final condition attached to effective praying. In one sense it is but another aspect of the previous condition.

6. A forgiving spirit

"And whenever you stand praying, forgive, if you have anything against any one; so that your Father also who is in heaven may forgive you your trespasses" (Mark 11:25). "So if you are offering your gift at the altar, and there remember that your brother has something against you, leave your gift there before the altar and go; first be reconciled to your brother, and then come and offer your gift" (Matthew 5:23, 24).

An unforgiving spirit toward a brother or sister in Christ ruins, not only fellowship with that individual, but also our fellowship with the Lord. This sin inevitably precludes our abiding in Christ, which in turn precludes our knowing His will. Thus these conditions of prayer are not separate and arbitrary conditions as though laid down by a capricious God. Rather they are like the beads of a necklace held together by one thread —that of holiness, without which there is no possibility of fellowship with man or with God.

"The prayer of a righteous man has great power in its effects" (James 5:16). Who can begin to measure the

103

power of prayer? Who can begin to estimate its effect upon history? Prayer is the greatest power on earth. And wherever there is great power, there must be many safeguards so that power will not be abused.

Christ gives no greater privilege to His church than the privilege of being "priests unto God." How eagerly we should covet a really effective prayer ministry and how obviously this will be concerned with the evangelization of the world—the extension of the kingdom of Jesus Christ. Surely no price will be too great to pay, no conditions too stringent to observe, that we may be found in this most strategic of all ministries in this tremendous period in the history of the world.

Chapter 8: **Missions and Money**

T̲HE INCOME of Protestant foreign mission boards in North America was almost $170,000,000 in 1959 and will be higher by 1961.[1]

By any standard this is a lot of money. Keeping a modern missionary in active service is costly, as indeed it is costly to keep a modern soldier in the front lines. Even before he actually begins his missionary work, there are many expenses to be paid in connection with his ordinary living—travel, food, rent, education of children, missionary services, language training, etc. In addition, modern missionary work in many cases demands tremendous expenditure on items such as airplanes, radio studios, correspondence courses, schools, hospitals, etc. No wonder that mission boards are always in need of money.

[1] There are 42,250 Protestant missionaries in the world today. The total number of North American Protestant missionaries in the world is 27,219. The income of North American agencies for 1959 (the last year for which we have figures) was $169,884,082.98. From this income 54.1% was for the development of foreign missions of the National Council of the Churches of Christ in the U.S.A. (oriented toward the World Council of Churches) and this group comprises 38% of the total missionary force from North America.

Missionary Research Library Occasional Bulletin November, 1960.

Not every Christian will find a place on the mission field itself to serve the Lord. But every Christian can make a vital contribution by praying and by the giving of money. We do not give, however, simply because there is need for financial help.

God could have planned the evangelization of the world without our contributing a cent. His resources are limitless, "For every beast of the forest is mine, the cattle on a thousand hills . . . If I were hungry, I would not tell you; for the world and all that is in it is mine" (Psalm 50:10, 12). The fact that God permits us to give of our money to accomplish His work on earth is a measure of His condescension. And there are deep-seated reasons for our ministry of giving—reasons that involve our own benefit as well as the extension of the kingdom of God.

Our giving—why we give, how we give, how much we give—also reveals much about our basic attitude toward God.

How do we measure generosity? How much of what we have belongs to God? Does spiritual blessing lead to generous material giving? Does giving lead to spiritual blessing? How should we give? These are some of the questions that we shall try to answer in this chapter.

1. *God's possessions*

"Moses said . . . I will stretch out my hands to the Lord; the thunder will cease, and there will be no more hail, *that you may know that the earth is the Lord's*"

(Exodus 9:29). "The land shall not be sold in perpetuity, for *the land is mine*" (Leviticus 25:23). "But who am I, and what is my people, that we should be able thus to offer willingly? For all things come from thee, and of thy own have we given thee" (I Chronicles 29:14). "*The earth is the Lord's* and the fulness thereof, the world and those who dwell therein" (Psalm 24:1). ". . . and I will shake all nations, so that the treasures of all nations shall come in, and I will fill this house with splendor, says the Lord of hosts. *The silver is mine,* and *the gold is mine,* says the Lord of hosts" (Haggai 2:7, 8). ". . . thus says the Lord, he who created you . . . who formed you . . . I have redeemed you; I have called you by name, *you are mine*" (Isaiah 43:1). "Know that the Lord is God! *It is he that made us,* and *we are his*; we are his people, and the sheep of his pasture" (Psalm 100:3).

The Scripture clearly, definitely, and repeatedly states that the whole earth, and everything and everybody on it, belong to God and are His by right of creation. Any thinking concerning the stewardship of our material possessions must begin with this premise.

2. *Our possessions?*

In the Old Testament the people of God were taught to give one-tenth of their possessions, or a tithe, to God. This practice is strongly advocated by many Bible teachers today. Is it right to assume that one-tenth of what we have belongs to God while the other

107

nine-tenths belongs to us? "If we live, we live to the
Lord, and if we die, we die to the Lord; so then,
whether we live or whether we die, we are the Lord's"
(Romans 14:8). ". . . You are not your own; you were
bought with a price . . ." (I Corinthians 6:19, 20). "I
appeal to you therefore, brethren, by the mercies of God,
to present your bodies as a living sacrifice, holy and
acceptable to God, which is your spiritual worship"
(Romans 12:1).

Thus too great an emphasis upon tithing can be dangerous; it may blind us to the truth that every cent we
have, every faculty we possess, every hour we live belongs entirely and completely to God. To think, even
subconsciously, that nine-tenths of what we own belongs to us is to be utterly ignorant of the standard of
the New Testament. The Apostle Paul referred again
and again to the fact that he was a "bond slave" of
Jesus Christ. A slave is one who possesses nothing for
himself, but who is possessed entirely by another.

This is the second fact that we must grasp and apply
if we are to understand the nature of true missionary
stewardship.

3. How does the Bible measure generosity?

In considering the subject of generosity, we must
turn at once to two passages of Scripture—one in the
Old Testament and one in the New Testament.

And Araunah said, "Why has my lord the king come
to his servant?" David said, "To buy the threshing

floor of you, in order to build an altar to the Lord, that the plague may be averted from the people." Then Araunah said to David, "Let my lord the king take and offer up what seems good to him; here are the oxen for the burnt offering, and the threshing sledges and the yokes of the oxen for the wood. All this, O king, Araunah gives to the king." And Araunah said to the king, "The Lord your God accept you." But the king said to Araunah, "No, but I will buy it of you for a price; I will not offer burnt offerings to the Lord my God which cost me nothing." So David bought the threshing floor and the oxen for fifty shekels of silver. And David built there an altar to the Lord, and offered burnt offerings and peace offerings. So the Lord heeded supplications for the land, and the plague was averted from Israel (II Samuel 24:21-25).

"And (Jesus) sat down opposite the treasury, and watched the multitude putting money into the treasury. Many rich people put in large sums. And a poor widow came, and put in two copper coins, which make a penny. And he called his disciples to him, and said to them, "Truly, I say to you, this poor widow has put in more than all those who are contributing to the treasury. For they all contributed out of their abundance; but she out of her poverty has put in everything she had, her whole living" (Mark 12:41-44).

In both these incidents emphasis is placed, not upon *what* is given to the Lord but on the *cost* of the giving. Generosity to God is measured, not by the amount of the gift, but by the amount that remains after the gift is given. The intrinsic worth of the bullocks was no greater because David rather than Araunah paid the

109

price for them. But David had seen the principle that giving to God must cost the giver something.

When Jesus sat beside the treasury with His disciples some thousand years later, He had something to teach them—something of paramount importance that contradicted what they had been taught to believe all their lives. As they watched, many rich people dropped large sums of money into the treasury. In the midst of this display of wealth, a poor woman put in two copper coins, the smallest coins in circulation at that time. Jesus' comment on her action, by human standards, was nonsense: "The widow has put in more than all those."

Actually, it is our human standards that are nonsense! "They . . . contributed out of their abundance; but she . . . put in everything she had." How much money was received into the treasury that day we shall never know. Doubtless it was extremely useful to those responsible for the upkeep of the temple. But so far as God was concerned, Jesus brushed aside much that was given with the phrase "out of their abundance." It was what would not be missed; it involved no sacrifice. It was worth nothing.

How devastating this is for us today!

Now let us look at another short passage in the Old Testament.

"Thus says the Lord of hosts: This people say the time has not yet come to rebuild the house of the Lord." Then the word of the Lord came by Haggai the prophet, "Is it a time for you yourselves to dwell in

your paneled houses, while this house lies in ruins?"
(Haggai 1:2-4).

The prophet is complaining that while God's house
lies in ruins the people are living in luxurious homes
with ornate furnishings. The incongruity of God's people spending lavishly on their own homes while neg-
lecting God's house was more than the prophet could
bear. But evidently it seemed very normal to the people
concerned. What Haggai would say about our homes
and our stewardship today is not too hard to imagine.
It would doubtless be blistering.

In measuring our generosity to the work of the Lord
our basic inquiry must be: "What is this costing me?
What am I denying myself that I might give to the
work of the Lord? Is this 'out of my abundance' or is
it 'out of my poverty'?" I will measure it less in terms
of what I give than in terms of what I have left after I
have given.

By this standard very few of us have begun to learn
true Biblical generosity. In our complacent and comfortable society we do not yet understand the meaning
of sacrifice, much less do we practice it.

4. *How much should I give?*

Basic to true Christian giving, as we have seen, is the
premise that everything belongs to God. But much of
what we have must be spent upon our own legitimate
needs. How much, then, should we give to the work of
the Lord?

111

For most of my adult life I have made a practice of giving at least one-tenth to the work of the Lord even during periods when it has been extremely hard to do so. Tithing is a very useful guide . . . but only a guide!

I have met people so poor that it did not seem to me God expected them to tithe; although I must add that I have never seen an adult in North America of whom I felt this to be true. On the other hand, I have met many Christians who were so wealthy that one-tenth of their income given to the Lord would be totally inadequate. For such a person to think that a tithe is sufficient is tantamount to treating God as they would a waiter—to giving Him a tip rather than an expression of love and of loyalty. Such giving must surely be an insult to God who "owns the cattle on a thousand hills" and who "so loved . . . that he gave his only Son."

We shall find out how much we should give in the same way that we find out how much time we should give in prayer. God deals with us as individuals and will guide us in that way, but He will do so according to the Biblical principles mentioned in this chapter. We can expect to find God's will for our giving. We dare not presume to find God's will for the giving of other people. If we are indulging our wants by giving relatively little to the work of the Lord, if our giving does not involve us in direct sacrifice, then our giving is inadequate by the standards of the New Testament. However generous we may seem to be in the eyes of others, we shall certainly not be generous in the eyes of God.

112

5. *Is generosity a consequence of spiritual blessing?*

The second chapter of Acts is a highly significant one in the Scriptures. It describes the events of the day in which the Church was born and, in verses 41 through 47, the conduct of those who became members of the Church that day. It is significant that one of the first results of the blessing of Pentecost was a change in the believers' attitudes toward their possessions.

> And all who believed were together and had all things in common; and they sold their possessions and goods and distributed them to all, as any had need (Acts 2:44, 45).

> Now the company of those who believed were of one heart and soul, and no one said that any of the things which he possessed was his own, but they had everything in common . . . There was not a needy person among them, for as many as were possessors of lands or houses sold them, and brought the proceeds of what was sold and laid it at the apostles' feet; and distribution was made to each as any had need (Acts 4:32-35).

Spiritual blessing immediately revealed itself in the attitude of the disciples toward material goods. The very things that a few days previously they would have said were indispensable—their possessions, their goods, their property—these things they sold that they might distribute the proceeds to the poor and needy who were in the Church. The Lord may not lead us to emulate their example exactly, but at least we are shown the

113

principle that spiritual blessing leads to material generosity.

The Apostle Paul includes an interesting passage on the Church in Thessalonica in his second letter to the Corinthians.

> We want you to know, brethren, about the grace of God which has been shown in the churches of Macedonia, for in a severe test of affliction, their abundance of joy and their extreme poverty have overflowed in a wealth of liberality on their part. For they gave according to their means, as I can testify, and beyond their means, of their own free will, begging us earnestly for the favor of taking part in the relief of the saints—and this, not as we expected, but first they gave themselves to the Lord and to us by the will of God (II Corinthians 8:1-5).

One more incident—this time from the life of our Lord concerning the woman who brought an alabaster flask of ointment.

> And Jesus answering said to him, "Simon, I have something to say to you." And he answered, "What is it, Teacher?" "A certain creditor had two debtors; one owed five hundred denarii, and the other fifty. When they could not pay, he forgave them both. Now which of them will love him more?" Simon answered, "The one, I suppose, to whom he forgave more." And he said to him, "You have judged rightly." Then turning toward the woman he said to Simon, "Do you see this woman? I entered your house, you gave me no water for my feet, but she has wet my feet with her tears

and wiped them with her hair. You gave me no kiss, but from the time I came in she has not ceased to kiss my feet. You did not anoint my head with oil, but she has anointed my feet with ointment. Therefore I tell you, her sins, which are many, are forgiven, for she loved much; but he who is forgiven little, loves little (Luke 7:40-47).

If there is in our lives no real desire to give to the Lord and to give generously, it may very well be an indication of the poverty of our own spiritual experience.

6. *Does generosity to the Lord's work guarantee material prosperity?*

Very frequently I have heard it said, particularly in missionary conferences, "God is no man's debtor. If you are generous to God He will look after your needs." The impression very clearly given is that if we do our part for the work of God, God will look after us more than adequately; that our putting Him first in the matter of stewardship is not mere generosity, it is a wise investment. Is this necessarily true?

No man gave more consistently of his possessions and of himself than the Apostle Paul, yet he could write about himself: "To the present hour we hunger and thirst, we are ill-clad and buffeted and homeless, and we labor, working with our own hands . . ." (I Corinthians 4:11, 12). The Apostle Paul put the Lord first and the Lord did bless him richly and continually, but

115

it certainly did not lead to a life of affluence, luxury, and comfort.

If we seek first the kingdom of God, other things that we need will be added (Matthew 6:33). God has promised to supply all of our needs, but this cannot be construed as meaning that financial giving on our part will inevitably lead to a great financial return.

It must be stated, however, that to withhold our money from the work of the Lord may result in chastisement from the Lord in the form of financial privation. "Another withholds what he should give, and only suffers want" (Proverbs 11:24).

> "Is it a time for yourselves to dwell in your paneled houses, while this house lies in ruins? Now therefore thus says the Lord of hosts: Consider how you have fared. You have sown much, and harvested little; you eat, but you never have enough; you drink, but you never have your fill; you clothe yourselves, but no one is warm; and he who earns wages earns wages to put them into a bag with holes" (Haggai 1:4-6).

7. *Does giving bring spiritual blessing?*

"A liberal man will be enriched, and one who waters will himself be watered" (Proverbs 11:25). "You are cursed with a curse, for you are robbing me; the whole nation of you. Bring the full tithes into the storehouse, that there may be food in my house; and thereby put me to the test, says the Lord of hosts, if I will not open the windows of heaven for you and pour down for you an overflowing blessing" (Malachi 3:9-10). "Give, and

116

it will be given to you; good measure, pressed down, shaken together, running over . . ." (Luke 6:38). "The point is this: he who sows sparingly will also reap sparingly, and he who sows bountifully will also reap bountifully. Each one must do as he has made up his mind, not reluctantly or under compulsion, for God loves a cheerful giver" (II Corinthians 9:6, 7).

Whatever may be our conclusions as to whether God blesses us in a material way when we give to His service, there can certainly be no doubt that when we give to Him generously He blesses us in spiritual ways. Perhaps this is one of the reasons why so many of us know so little of God's bounty, because we have shared with Him so little of our own. No wonder, also, that the Apostle Paul writes to the Philippians and says, "Not that I seek the gift; but I seek the fruit which increases to your credit" (Philippians 4:17). The Apostle Paul saw that there was a tremendous link between financial giving and spiritual growth, and what he coveted for the Philippian Christians more than anything else was not the proceeds of their generosity so far as others were concerned, but the overflowing grace that would show itself in their lives if they contributed generously to the work of the Lord and to their fellow Christians.

Let us be quite sure that we take this lesson to heart, and not merely to heart but also into practice.

8. *How should I give to foreign missions?*

The Bible is surprisingly full and frank in its treatment of giving and fund raising. Consider, for example, the words of Jesus Christ.

> Thus, when you give alms, sound no trumpet before you, as the hypocrites do in the synagogues and in the streets, that they may be praised by men. Truly, I say to you, they have their reward. But when you give alms, do not let your left hand know what your right hand is doing, so that your alms may be in secret; and your Father who sees in secret will reward you (Matthew 6:2-4).

> Heal the sick, raise the dead, cleanse lepers, cast out demons. You received without pay, give without pay (Matthew 10:8).

Free as he was from the vulgarity that sometimes characterizes the raising of money for foreign missions in our twentieth century, the Apostle Paul nevertheless pulled no punches when he spoke to believers about the old question of their financial responsibility.

> Now concerning the contribution for the saints: as I directed the churches of Galatia, so you also are to do. On the first day of every week, each of you is to put something aside and store it up, as he may prosper, so that contributions need not be made when I come. And when I arrive, I will send those whom you accredit by letter to carry your gift to Jerusalem (I Corinthians 16:1-3).

> Each one must do as he has made up his mind, not reluctantly or under compulsion, for God loves a cheerful giver (II Corinthians 9:7).

118

Perhaps the three points that we need to make from these various passages of Scripture are as follows:

1. The Lord expects us to give, not with a begrudging spirit but with a sense of joy that we are allowed to contribute to His work and to express our fellowship with others who are in His work. A begrudging spirit about money reveals a begrudging spirit in the whole of our response to the love and generosity of God.

2. Such giving should be systematic and methodical. The Apostle Paul makes it clear that each man must make up his mind before God what he is to give and then set it aside each week. The exact method that should be used we are not told, and it should not matter. But the fact that there should be some method is clearly stressed. Our giving should not be haphazard, based upon sentimentality or emotion, but systematic.

3. Our giving should be unostentatious. "Do not let your left hand know what your right hand is doing" says the Scripture. In other words, any giving that is based upon the fact that men shall see us is utterly unavailing so far as the opinion of God is concerned. Jesus Christ dismisses this with a phrase, "Verily they have their reward."

We see then that one of the priceless privileges of the Christian is to contribute to the work of the Lord, by actual service himself, by the wonderful ministry of prayer, and by the ministry of finances. It is unfortunately true that much of the work of the Lord is hampered or spoiled through the shortage of money. It

119

is also true that the giving of our money is, in addition to being a help to the work of God, an immeasurable blessing to those who give. We have no need to feel embarrassed in talking about money. The Apostle Paul did it frankly and openly and frequently.

Now we need to ask ourselves: Is our love for the Lord revealing itself in the stewardship of our possessions? Is our concern for foreign missions being translated into positive terms in the matter of finance?

It is very easy to say that we will start to give when once we have some money, but as with all disciplines in the Christian life, including those of time and prayer, we have to begin giving however much or little we may seem to have. It is during the years when we are students that lifelong habits are formed. It is therefore imperative that we face up now to the challenge and responsibility and privilege of giving of our substance to the work of the Lord overseas. Our personal budgets, our chapter budgets should be planned so that we are making the maximum impact for the evangelization of the world through the very money that the Lord has entrusted to us.

Chapter 9: **Missionary Qualifications**

A MISSIONARY from the Orient writes:

I was handed a Singapore newspaper with an editorial in bold face on the first page that immediately caught my attention. It contained a criticism of missionary education, charging that its purpose is to "educate the natives to accept Western ideas with the Christian faith so that they would be more amenable to the white man's rule." The closing paragraph presented a significant challenge, "Can the Christian Church in Asian lands, immersed in Western ways and ideas, compete with the traditional Eastern faith? Can it overcome Asian prejudice against the Western way of doing things, or will Christianity in course of time retreat with the receding tide of Western imperialism from Asia?"

The answer to these questions may in a large degree depend upon the quality of Christian leadership that is being prepared in the Church today. Success or failure of missionary work will depend, not so much upon the amount of work accomplished by the missionary himself, but upon the spiritual qualifications of the national leaders who are influenced by his fellowship with them.

The director of a mission working in Latin America

writes, "In my opinion we have to learn to minister in an unfriendly world, and Cuba is a good testing place for us."

The director of a mission working among Muslims in Africa writes concerning the health qualifications needed in new missionaries to his country: "We should look for a rugged, robust fitness . . . although I am quite sure that in the homeland you could live with certain disabilities, I am of the opinion we should accept those who would approach a Marine Corps fitness." Concerning temperament in missionaries, he writes, "I would strongly recommend that if there is the slightest indication of such weakness in the early stages of dealing with a candidate, he should not be encouraged to continue his application." Concerning spiritual maturity, he writes, "My personal feeling is that the modern set-up of the Bible schools and seminaries, although basically good and unquestionably sending a large number of fine young people into the mission field, has very serious weaknesses. There never was an epoch in which it was easier to acquire knowledge. Young missionaries these days have tremendous academic preparations, but too often such knowledge remains in the theoretical stage, even though they come out to do battle on the mission field. In order to attack this entrenched problem of Islam, we need men and women of rugged spirituality."

There are many and differing technical qualifications needed among missionaries today in fields such as radio, aeronautics, linguistics, artwork, medicine, teaching, journalism, etc., but these quotations remind us that missionary qualifications are less concerned with what a missionary does than with what a missionary is.

The great expansion of missionary work at the close of the last century took place at a time when the prestige of the white man was high and the color of his skin was enough to guarantee a respectful hearing. It was dangerously possible to be patronizing, and for some of the imperialism of the Western World to rub off on the missionary.

Those days have gone forever, and it is well that they have. Ideological, cultural, and racial developments of the last fifteen years have brought about a climate of change and tension that demands a superior breed of missionary.

What are the qualities of the new missionaries demanded by the world situation today?

Strangely enough, they are not *new* qualities, for they are as old as the Apostle Paul himself. Neither are these qualities demanded merely of Christians who would serve the Lord abroad but of all who would please the Lord whether at home or overseas. These qualities are demanded by world conditions, but first and primarily by the New Testament. Some of them are as follows:

1. *Humility*

A main missionary task today is to train nationals for

123

leadership in the younger churches. The ability to produce leadership on the foreign field depends on the degree to which the missionary is prepared to work as a brother and a partner, and this demands a high standard of humility. It is not difficult to be humble with those who are obviously our juniors and our inferiors. Neither is it difficult to be humble with those who are obviously our seniors and superiors. But the real test of humility is the way in which we treat our equals.

In many situations the foreign missionary is called to negotiate with officials in countries who have recently received their independence and have a strong sense of national pride. In many cases the local officials may be bitter toward the white man. To radiate the love of Christ in such a situation demands humility.

In countries where the Church has become fully indigenous and national leadership is established, there are many instances where the missionary will be working under the leadership and supervision of a national. For such a situation to be harmonious great humility is demanded on the part of both nationals and missionaries.

The Apostle Paul was by temperament highly individualistic, fiercely proud of his independence, born to lead, a man who even before his conversion seemed to dominate situations. Yet such was the transformation in his life that he subsequently delighted to refer to himself as a "slave of Jesus Christ."

"Slave" is an ugly word. There is no room for pride

124

in the life of a slave. There is no liberty in the life of a slave. He has no rights. He is owned by his master as completely as one of the domestic animals, yet this is a term that the Apostle Paul applies to himself again and again.

But he uses this term not merely in connection with his attitude to Jesus Christ, but also his attitude to others. "For though I am free from all men, I have made myself a slave to all, that I might win the more" (I Corinthians 9:19). "For what we preach is not ourselves, but Jesus Christ as Lord, with ourselves as your servants for Jesus' sake" (II Corinthians 4:5).

Before any man can serve the Lord in the way it will please Him, the Lord has to make clear to him his own unworthiness and lack of qualifications for the task.

To many this experience takes place at the very beginning of their encounter with Jesus Christ. Thus it was with the Apostle Paul. "Now as he journeyed he approached Damascus, and suddenly a light from heaven flashed about him. And he fell to the ground and heard a voice . . . and he said, 'Who are you, Lord?' " (Acts 9:3-5). The contrast between verse one, "But Saul, still breathing threats and murder against the disciples . . ." and verse eight, "Saul arose from the ground; and when his eyes were opened, he could see nothing; so they led him by the hand . . ." is significant and symbolic of a change that reached down into the deepest part of his being and made him the missionary par excellence.

125

His natural abilities, his training, his religion, his sincerity—all these great gifts united to make him only a persecutor of the Church of Jesus Christ. This encounter with Jesus Christ alone made him the missionary that he was. Arthur Glasser has said, "That day he got on his face in the dust and he never got up again."

Similarly, with the prophet Isaiah, ". . . I saw the Lord sitting upon a throne, high and lifted up . . . And I said: 'Woe is me! For I am lost; for I am a man of unclean lips, and I dwell in the midst of a people of unclean lips; for my eyes have seen the King, the Lord of hosts!' . . And I heard the voice of the Lord saying, 'Whom shall I send, and who will go . . . ?' Then I said, 'Here I am! Send me.' And he said, 'Go . . .' " (Isaiah 6:1, 5, 8, 9).

This sense of unworthiness and disqualification characterized the servants of the Lord in the Old Testament. When the Lord appeared to Jeremiah and appointed him a prophet, the response of the prophet was: "Then I said, 'Ah, Lord God! Behold, I do not know how to speak, for I am only a youth' " (Jeremiah 1:6).

It is significant to note that one of the steps that our Lord took in dealing with the Apostle Peter in making him such an outstanding disciple was the way in which he overruled Peter's great failure and denial to bring him to a place of brokenness.

Then they seized him and led him away, bringing him into the high priest's house. Peter followed at a distance; and when they had kindled a fire in the middle

126

of the courtyard and sat down together, Peter sat among them. Then a maid, seeing him as he sat in the light and gazing at him, said, "This man also was with him." But he denied it, saying, "Woman, I do not know him." And a little later some one else saw him and said, "You also are one of them." But Peter said, "Man, I am not." And after an interval of about an hour still another insisted, saying, "Certainly this man also was with him; for he is a Galilean." But Peter said, "Man, I do not know what you are saying." And immediately, while he was still speaking, the cock crowed. And the Lord turned and looked at Peter. And Peter remembered the word of the Lord, how he had said to him, "Before the cock crows today, you will deny me three times." And he went out and wept bitterly (Luke 22:54-62).

With the prophet Isaiah and with the Apostle Paul, this sense of inadequacy came only after a vision of the glory of God. "At midday, O king, I saw on the way a light from heaven, brighter than the sun, shining round me and those who journeyed with me" (Acts 26:13). A true sense of the glory of God will inevitably give to us a true perspective of ourselves, revealing fully to us our own spiritual bankruptcy. "Blessed are the poor in spirit, for theirs is the kingdom of heaven" (Matthew 5:3).

The supreme example of this kind of service was set by Jesus Christ himself. "Jesus, knowing that the Father had given all things into his hands, and that he had come from God and was going to God, rose from supper,

127

laid aside his garments, and girded himself with a towel. Then he poured water into a basin, and began to wash the disciples' feet, and to wipe them with the towel with which he was girded" (John 13:3-5). "Jesus, knowing that the Father had given all things into his hands . . . girded himself with a towel." What a magnificent example of humility, of the kind of service He asks of His followers.

> Have this mind among yourselves, which you have in Christ Jesus, who, though he was in the form of God, did not count equality with God a thing to be grasped, but emptied himself, taking the form of a servant, being born in the likeness of men. And being found in human form he humbled himself and became obedient unto death, even death on a cross (Philippians 2:5-8).

"Come to me, all who labor and are heavy-laden, and I will give you rest. Take my yoke upon you, and learn from me; for I am gentle and lowly in heart, and you will find rest for your souls" (Matthew 11:28, 29).

In these Scriptures we have set before us, not merely the example of Jesus Christ, but the exhortation that His followers conform to His pattern. Such conformance is the antidote to pride of race, pride of color, pride of position. Only thus will the followers of Jesus Christ minister in His Name and by His Spirit in this generation. Only thus will we be able to identify with the people to whom we go, as it is imperative that we identify in these days.

128

2. Boldness and perseverance

These qualities are a necessary complement to the quality of humility. In the Second World War, a general remarked, "The best soldier is not the one who is braver than others, but the one who is brave for longer than others." What is needed in spiritual conflict as in earthly battles is not merely dash and daring, but perseverance and doggedness in the face of discouragements and danger.

"May you be strengthened with all power, according to his glorious might, for all endurance and patience with joy, giving thanks to the Father . . ." (Colossians 1:11, 12). This prayer of Paul for the Christians at Colossae makes it clear that Christian courage is not merely the sparkling variety, but the abiding variety.

Boldness and perseverance are demanded today in every aspect of the work and life of an effective missionary: in combating entrenched forms of hostile religions and ideologies; in the discipline of learning a language; in the adaptation to what in many cases is a very much lower standard of living; and in the ability to face death itself calmly and in true faith. While it is true that the number of fatalities among Caucasian missionaries has been relatively few in the past few years, we need to remind ourselves that probably in the last twenty-five years more people have been martyred for their faith in Jesus Christ throughout the world than in any other comparable period of history. Indeed, some would say

129

that more have been killed in the last twenty-five years than in the whole of the rest of history. It is imperative that we remember the standard of devotion to Jesus Christ is that we shall send forth workers who "love not their lives unto death." Their attitude toward death will be reflected in their attitude toward life. We need Christians today who are prepared to live dangerously for Jesus Christ, and to do so in a disciplined way.

Part of our ineffectiveness at home and on the campus stems from unwillingness to bear reproach for the sake of Jesus Christ. Very frequently a sneer, a derogatory remark, a suggestion that we are uninformed and bigoted is enough to silence us in our campus situations. This really means that we are more concerned with the opinions of men than we are with Jesus Christ's opinion of our life and testimony. "Nevertheless many even of the authorities believed in him, but for fear of the Pharisees they did not confess it, lest they should be put out of the synagogue: for they loved the praise of men more than the praise of God" (John 12:42, 43).

> Hence I remind you to rekindle the gift of God that is within you through the laying on of my hands; for God did not give us a spirit of timidity but a spirit of power and love and self-control. Do not be ashamed then of testifying to our Lord, nor of me his prisoner, but take your share of suffering for the gospel in the power of God (II Timothy 1:6-8).

"You then, my son, be strong in the grace that is in

130

Christ Jesus . . . Take your share of suffering as a good soldier of Christ Jesus" (II Timothy 2:1, 3).

This needed boldness and perseverance result not from natural flair or talent but from a spiritual gift. "God did not give us the spirit of timidity, but the spirit of power . . ." It is significant that immediately after Pentecost the word "boldness" is applied again and again to the lives and ministry of the apostles. Thus in Acts 4:13: "Now when they saw the boldness of Peter and John, and perceived that they were uneducated, common men, they wondered; and they recognized that they had been with Jesus." And when they had prayed, the place in which they were gathered together was shaken; and they were all filled with the Holy Spirit and spoke the word of God with boldness" (Acts 4:31).

This boldness and perseverance, then, is not something we work up ourselves, with which we are endowed or not as the case may be, but a spiritual grace. This is one of the fruits of the Holy Spirit, and we must trust the Lord for this grace to be manifested in our own life and testimony at home or abroad.

3. Compatibility

It is obvious that, in addition to a healthy body and a well-educated mind, temperament plays a large part in a missionary's life. A mission board is always anxious to determine whether or not a potential missionary has the ability to work with and understand others. Far too many failures on the mission field have resulted from a

131

missionary who is "temperamental." Some people have personalities that make it very hard for them to adjust to other missionaries and to nationals. But we can be glad that Christ is a mender of temperaments. There is no reason for any Christian who has an awkward temperament to assume that he can do nothing about correcting it. Mission boards certainly should not exclude the possibility of the Lord changing a difficult temperament, but they will want clear evidence before the person sails to the field that this change has in fact taken place and that the candidate's contribution on the field will be positive rather than negative.

Moodiness, bad temper, and jealousy are serious problems in any Christian, but to see the way that such deficiencies can be exploited by Satan on the mission field is almost frightening.

There are great differences in personality which are God-given and which retain their distinctiveness when we become Christians. God does not abolish our individual characteristics at conversion. Rather He plants within us His Holy Spirit, refining our personalities and making our bodies temples of the living God. The Apostle Paul tells us that ". . . the fruit of the Spirit is love, joy, peace, patience, kindness, goodness, faithfulness, gentleness, self-control . . ." (Galatians 5:22, 23).

> For this very reason make every effort to supplement your faith with virtue, and virtue with knowledge, and knowledge with self-control, and self-control with steadfastness, and steadfastness with godliness, and

godliness with brotherly affection, and brotherly affection with love. For if these things are yours and abound, they keep you from being ineffective or unfruitful in the knowledge of our Lord Jesus Christ. For whoever lacks these things is blind and shortsighted and has forgotten that he was cleansed from his old sins (II Peter 1:5-9).

Basically, of course, Christianity is a religion of intolerance. So it came into conflict with the Roman Empire in its early days and with various other states throughout history. But we need people on the mission field who will learn to differentiate between things that are important and things that are fundamental. There is a danger of holding opinions and calling them principles. The very basis of unity is a willingness to concede to others a right to their own opinions on points of interpretation which are not central. Even more than this is involved. There will come times when we have to come face to face with an opposing religion and have to expose error. How many examples have we had of evangelicals who have spoken the truth but have failed to do so in love. The Apostle Paul was always forthright and demanding in the message that he preached, but he was conciliatory in the spirit in which he preached it. How we need to learn this lesson today. "And the Lord's servant must not be quarrelsome but kindly to every one, an apt teacher, forbearing, correcting his opponents with gentleness. God may perhaps grant that they will repent and come to know the truth" (II Timothy 2:24, 25).

133

4. *Empathy*

According to Webster's New World Dictionary, College Edition, empathy is "the projection of one's own personality into the personality of another in order to understand him better." Henry Drummond once said of D. L. Moody that "he was certainly not the greatest brain in the world, but he was one of the greatest human beings." It was the very quality of his humanity that made it so easy for him to know other people and to be known by them.

Spurgeon defined fellowship as "the willingness to know and to be known." To be prepared to know other people involves the willingness to be interested in other people, to take time to cultivate them, to be quiet and listen to them, to attempt to understand them. To know others is difficult enough in our own culture, but very much more difficult in another culture which may be very different from our own. To be willing to know somebody else is quite impossible if I am self-centered, always and only interested in things that concern my ego.

In the second half of the definition, Spurgeon speaks of the "willingness to be known." Basic to true Christian fellowship is honesty and an openness with other people, a transparency which comes when we live to God and make no attempt either to keep up a front (which derives from pride and fear of being known for what we truly are) or even to protect ourselves from misunderstanding or hostility (our concern to be loved eclipsed by our readiness to love others).

This quality will show itself first of all in my relationships with other Christians. In the early chapters of the Acts of the Apostles, it is obvious that one of the first fruits of the filling of the Holy Spirit was a remarkable degree of fellowship among Christians. The Apostle John discusses this matter fully and repeatedly in his first letter. "But he who hates his brother is in the darkness and walks in the darkness, and does not know where he is going, because the darkness has blinded his eyes" (I John 2:11). "Beloved, if God so loved us, we also ought to love one another. No man has ever seen God; if we love one another, God abides in us and his love is perfected in us" (I John 4:11, 12).

Empathy will also be manifested in relationships with those who are not Christians and who may be of a different race. Studies in anthropology are tremendously helpful in adjusting to those of another race, and study in this field is to be highly recommended. At the same time it is important to remember that real, God-given concern for other people and real and ruthless dealing with self-centeredness in our own lives will do much to make it possible for us to "project our own personality into the personality of another in order to understand him better."

5. *A sense of call*

We are all different personalities, and thus the call of

135

God to service comes to each of us in a different way, for God treats us as the individuals we are.

There are some things to which all of us are called. We are all called to be "witnesses of Jesus Christ" (evident from the reading of the Acts of the Apostles). We are all called to be "filled with the Holy Spirit" (Ephesians 5:18). We are all called to show forth the "fruits of the Spirit." Whether we go abroad or stay at home, these are callings that we all have, whatever may be our paid occupation. But we are not all called to be foreign missionaries for Jesus Christ, and to go to the field without being called by Him is disastrous.

There are missionaries on the foreign field who have told me they went out of a sense of obligation, because they felt that it was the "done thing for every keen Christian to do."

A person is hardly likely to stand the disappointments of work abroad unless he is truly called by the Lord and equipped by Him. It should be mentioned that we ought to be just as cautious about a call to undertake any profession in the homeland as we are about foreign service. A call to foreign missionary service is not different in quality or quantity from the call to any other kind of occupation, be it that of housewife or engineer or faculty member. Generally, we should find God's will concerning service on the mission field in exactly the same way as we find His will in every other area of our lives. If we cultivate the practice of looking to Him to guide us in our daily affairs, then we shall find

His presence guiding us when it comes to the question of missionary service overseas.

The danger of going abroad without being called has been mentioned. The danger of too great passivity must also be brought to mind. To be a "special messenger" of Jesus Christ is a very great privilege. But the Apostle Paul has made it clear that we are permitted to covet such a gift: "And earnestly desire the spiritual gifts, especially that you may prophesy" (I Corinthians 14:1). To send ourselves to the foreign field would be presumptuous and disastrous; but, knowing ourselves as unqualified and unworthy, we may ask the Lord to give to us the gift of being a foreign missionary for His sake and for His glory.

6. Love

A Christian without love is like a reading lamp without a bulb. It may be an attractive ornament, but it is totally useless so far as its true function is concerned. I shall not soon forget the experience of meeting a missionary gifted in language, experienced in the ways of a country, loyal to his mission and senior in status, who as an effective missionary was totally useless because he had lost his love for those to whom God had sent him. It is easy to become cynical when surrounded by the unlovely and the unappreciative; and yet it is this compassion alone that can make us effective servants for Jesus Christ. "If I speak . . . if I have prophetic powers . . . understand all mysteries and all knowledge . . . if

137

I have all faith . . . but have not love, *I am nothing.* If I give . . . if I deliver my body to be burned, but have not love, I gain nothing" (I Corinthians 13:1-3).

The Apostle Paul was doing more here than giving good advice. He was articulating a basic fact in his own life and effectiveness.

> But we were gentle among you, like a nurse taking care of her children. So, being affectionately desirous of you, we were ready to share with you not only the gospel of God but also our own selves, because you had become very dear to us (I Thessalonians 2:7, 8).

This is the quality that alone can break down barriers of prejudice in our own hearts and break down prejudice in the hearts of those among whom God sends us to minister.

7. *Spiritual effectiveness*

This has been left until last, because it is the most important of all, and in many ways the most difficult of all to define. What is called for is not merely Biblical knowledge, but spiritual fervor and effectiveness. The Word of God makes it quite clear in the book of Revelation that the churches of Ephesus and Laodicea did not lack in their knowlege of the truth but in their walk of devotion to the Lord.

Today we have perhaps a higher standard of academic preparation for the mission field than ever before, but it is unfortunately true that there are very few

138

candidates whose prayer and conversation are such as to have a heartwarming quality.

The greatest failure in the Church's mission today is not the scarcity of missionaries, nor the shortage of money, nor the lack of prayer partners. These are rather symptoms of a deeper disorder. The great lack in the Church today is real spiritual power, the evidence and the confidence that God himself is at work in and through the lives of men. Above all else, we need men and women of spiritual power and vitality—a vitality that will reveal itself by the lives they lead and their influence on other men and women. If our lives have never had any impact on the course of another life, we may well ask ourselves if we know anything of true spiritual effectiveness. The ability to attain a certain professional competence, the ability to do a particular job well, is totally inadequate preparation for the mission field today. We need men who can work in the lives of other men; and these will be men who have begun so to work long before they ever left their own shores or, in many cases, their own campuses.

Robert I. Brown is the Deputy Field Director of the North Africa Mission. He says that near Tunis, the town in which he works, there is a mountain along the base of which is a road. Many people pass back and forth along the road; a few climb the mountain. At the beginning of the climb, they are not far removed in altitude from the passers-by along the road. But their direction is different, and their faces are set toward the mountain peak. Comments Mr. Brown: "We are not looking for men who have arrived at the top, but we are looking for those whose faces are set toward the mountain peak, whose lives show a determination to keep climbing."

"Therefore, brethren, pick out from among you seven men of good repute, full of the Spirit and of wisdom, whom we may appoint to this duty" (Acts 6:3). Our speaking, our praying, our giving, everything that we do and are will depend in the final analysis upon our ability to walk with God and to know the fullness of His Spirit resting on us and abiding in us. "Hence I remind you to rekindle the gift of God that is within you through the laying on of my hands" (II Timothy 1:6). How easily our spiritual fervor cools. How readily our spiritual effectiveness wanes. We must be continually on our guard, ruthlessly dealing with things that would intrude between our God and us. The habit of the daily quiet time is basic, but we must beware of the tendency for this to become merely an outward exercise. We must make sure that it becomes the habitual experience of intimate communion with the Lord day by day.

Humility, boldness and perseverance, compatibility, empathy, a sense of call, love, spiritual effectiveness. These are seven qualities that missions are looking for, and more important, that God is looking for. For His purpose is always the glory of God in the people of God. And this is man's peace.

Does this seem to be an exacting standard? It is the

New Testament standard—for missionaries, for all Christians. How do we measure up to such a standard?

These qualities are not natural endowments that we have or do not have; they are spiritual gifts and fruits, obtainable by every child of God. "Blessed are those who hunger and thirst for righteousness, for they shall be satisfied" (Matthew 5:6).

These qualities *are* obtainable—but only from their Source, only out of real desire, and only at a cost. They are never had at bargain prices from Him who paid an unfathomable price for us in the person of His Son. This God who is Lord of lords must be Lord of everything.

Epilogue

WHEN STACEY WOODS speaks of our being bought for a price, of the love of Christ constraining us to live no longer for ourselves but for Him, he often tells this story. It is one which he heard as a little boy, perched on the knee of a distinguished missionary who was visiting in his family home in Australia.

The missionary was John Alexander Clarke, and the incident he related to the expectant child occurred in the Belgian Congo some forty-five years ago, when life there was immeasurably more primitive even than it appears today.

Because hunting was their sole source of meat supply, Mr. Clarke used to go on safaris with his African boys. On one such safari they sighted a lion, but excitement yielded quickly to alarm as they observed the animal's prey: an African whom the lion was dragging off to devour. Fortunately Mr. Clarke was able to shoot and kill the beast. Seconds later he was at the side of the victim, who was still alive although in fearful condition—torn, lacerated, and delirious.

Mr. Clarke and his boys carried the wounded man back to the missionary's home. Weeks of careful nursing

143

followed, and at length, he was well enough to return to his home and tribe some distance away.

Months passed with no news heard or expected of his former patient. Late one afternoon when Mr. Clarke was seated on the veranda of his missionary home, he was surprised to see a little retinue of people emerging slowly from the forest on to the edge of the clearing in front of his house. He could discern a man who was obviously the leader, a number of women and children, followed by two cows, chickens, and some pigs.

The little retinue continued to approach his home, and Mr. Clarke rose to meet the leader at the edge of the veranda. There the African, a fine figure of a man, knelt before him.

"Bwana," he said. "Don't you recognize me?"

Suddenly Mr. Clarke realized that this was the man who some months before had been so desperately ill following the lion's attack. He was delighted to see him and welcomed him gladly, but was puzzled by the caravan of people and livestock that accompanied him.

The African drew himself up to his full height.

"It is the law of the forest and of my tribe, Bwana, that when a man has been attacked by a lion and has had his life saved by another, he no longer belongs to himself. He belongs to his savior. The lion was about to eat me, and you saved me. So here I am. All that I am and have belongs to you. My wives are your wives, my children are your children, my possessions are your possessions. I am your slave."

144

DATE DUE

OCT 3 '66			
OCT 17 '66			
NOV 28 '68			
DEC 13 '02			
Winkler			
APR 2 '74			
FEB 17 '75			
GAYLORD			PRINTED IN U.S.A.